We're Missing
the Point

We're Missing the Point

What's Wrong With the Orthodox Jewish Community and How to Fix It

להחזיר עטרה ליושנה

Gidon Rothstein

OUPRESS

NEW YORK

ISBN 978-1-60280-202-5

Layout: Marzel A.S — Jerusalem

Published by
OU Press
an imprint of the Orthodox Union
11 Broadway
New York, NY 10004
www.oupress.org
oupress@ou.org

Distributed by
KTAV Publishing House, Inc.
888 Newark Avenue, Suite 119
Jersey City, NJ 07306
Tel. (201) 963-9524
Fax. (201) 963-0102
www.ktav.com
orders@ktav.com

The author wishes to thank all those who have helped him arrive at this day, From HaKadosh Baruch Hu, to family, teachers, mentors, and friends. In particular, he notes the finanacial support and generosity of his family, of members of the post-Hashkamah Minyan Shiur at the Riverdale Jewish Center, and of the Bravmann Family.

Contents

Part 1

We're Missing the Point

Introduction

As a teenager, I would sometimes idly wonder about the embarrassment I would feel if, at the end of my life, I went up to Heaven for judgment and found the central figure of one of the other major world religions looking at me, shaking his head, and tsking sadly. Not a promising start for a reconsideration of Judaism, you might think, but bear with me for a moment.

As I grew older, I came to realize I wasn't so much pondering the truth of Judaism, but the possibility that, with all the sincerity in the world, I might have misunderstood (or been mistaught) what I was supposed to do. *That* concern, I confess, has not only stayed with me through the years, it has become stronger — the fear that many, if not most of us, sincerely struggling to fulfill God's Will, are nonetheless far off the mark, and that not because we are bad or weak, but because we do not even realize the basic parameters of what it means to serve God.

One small example of this came years ago, when I spoke to several rabbis and educators about working to make daily prayer more meaningful. The conversation would go something like this: "Shouldn't we strive to help people understand the words they're saying, to give them some sense of how to communicate with God, not just to rush through a fixed liturgy?" And the response I would get would go something like, "What do you want to criticize people for — here they are, dedicated enough to get up at 6 a.m. to go to *minyan*, and you want to tell them they're not really praying?" And I would say, to no avail, "Shouldn't our respect for their efforts spur us to want to help them have an actual conversation with God?"

In a nutshell, that is the goal of this book, only not just for prayer. I hope here to help all of us who sincerely want to relate to God productively see the basics of how to do so. The problem with claiming to do that is that many people never worried as I did, and are absolutely certain that they already know what God wants of them.

To some extent, that is because we tend to settle and stay with the vision of truth we accepted at an early point in our lives, without checking or adjusting. That helps us avoid a life of constant flux, lacking in fixed axioms or reference points, which would be unsettling and unproductive. The strategy fails, though, when the version of truth we chose misses vital points. This is, in my opinion, the case for much of Judaism today and the need for this book.

In short, my thesis is: We, many or most of us, are missing the point. God gave the world (Jews and non-Jews) a manual for how best to serve God, but few if any of us are even on the right track, let alone closing in on perfection in that service.

The good news is how easy the right track is to find; it mostly involves changing our frame of mind in two ways: 1) understanding that no matter how many commandments God gave, no matter how many different laws and customs those commandments have expanded to over the course of history, there is a central group of ideas that is supposed to be the focus of our efforts, that is supposed to be the shaping framework for all the other practices of the religion; and 2) recognizing that the Jewish system (as it applies to each human being, Jew and non-Jew) is both the *only* starting point for developing a legitimate closeness with God and also only the *starting* point, setting the parameters for a personal journey to be determined by each servant of God individually.

Let me also stress here and repeatedly throughout that even if I am completely correct, the fix needed to get back on track would not require *more* effort from Jews who are already trying hard, just a different kind and focus of effort. If we're putting in the time already, wouldn't it be great if we were doing it the way God has told us to?

It's Not Obvious

I am tempted to jump right in, to begin elaborating on what I just said. But I worry that, only a few paragraphs into our discussion, you are already tempted to lay the book aside, either because you find it too obvious, threatening, or both.

For those who find it obvious, let me note how different the words you just read are from what you tend to see elsewhere. For one simple statistic, less than one-tenth of one percent of the world's population accept the ideas I claim are the essential point of what Judaism tries to convey to humanity. That number is accurate even if we restrict our sample to adherents of the three monotheistic religions and not much higher if we look only at Jews.

Even among Orthodox Jews,[1] with whom I theoretically identify, I believe we will see that most such Jews either do not recognize or accept the ideas I lay out here or certainly do not give them the prominence they deserve. Many would insist Judaism is more about specific rituals than about being paragons of a certain worldview.

Watching the conduct of Judaism today, Jews' behavior today, in my experience, does not always express the system's clarity as to human beings' basic task: to worship God, to become closer to God, and to become more God-like, by refraining from certain abhorrent actions, performing certain commandments, which will help us build personal and creative ways to bring a certain

---

1. I mean the term Orthodox less as a denominational marker than as a synonym for those who strive to serve God as prescribed in the Written and Oral Laws and elaborated throughout Jewish history. If my words ring true for Conservative, Reform, Reconstructionist, non- or post-denominational Jews, and non-Jews, nothing would please me more. In trying to live up to my claim to be unequivocal, though, I accept that I will have to speak of Orthodox Jews and Judaism. Anyone willing to substitute the longer phrase "servant of God or observant of Torah and *mitzvot* as Jewish tradition always assumed" for each time I write "Orthodox" should do so, with my grateful thanks and appreciation.

worldview to our daily lives. From Jews' attitude towards Jewish law, we might not realize how few of the mechanisms for serving God are codified very exactly for Jews or non-Jews, and we would further not realize that the system obligates people to focus their life endeavors on the service of God, even when, perhaps especially when, not specifically commanded.

There are two reasons people might find my ideas threatening. As I said before, some people don't want to contemplate having to put even more into their religion than they already are. To them, I say again that adopting the ideas I record here does not call for any more effort, just a different kind. Others might suspect I will divert attention from what they see as the "real" focus of the religion; to them, I stress that much of this book will follow the strict discipline of presenting only those ideas that are unanimous in Jewish tradition, or very nearly so.

Before I get to that, let me suggest that the reason we do not see this in Jewish observance today is that most of us, Jewish or not, tend to be checklisters or ritualists. Checklisters limit religion to a list to check off and then leave it aside. In Jewish terms, such people attend synagogue on Shabbat, recite *Kiddush*, and have a meal in cognizance of the special day, but then feel free to do whatever they want until some other specifically legislated obligation comes around. Or, for another example, some Jews fulfill their various well-defined religious financial responsibilities (charity, supporting the local Jewish institutions), and then feel "free" to do whatever else with their money they wish.

Ritualist Jews are, in some sense, at the opposite end of the spectrum, in that they are focused on filling every moment of their lives with God's service. Where they differ from what I will try to show here is in focusing on exactly specified rituals as the only (or, certainly, the best) avenues for such service. For them, carrying a *lulav* is worship of God, as is sitting in a *sukkah* or eating kosher; once *halachah*, Jewish law, does not expressly define an act as obligated, they sense its religious value less. For many such Jews, the focus on *halachah* obscures other vital aspects of our religious development.

Either version, I am here to try to convince you, is not only not as good as it could be, it misses essential and indispensable aspects of what God sought from humanity. To rediscover that essence, I offer this book, in two parts. The first part argues that there *is* a core to Judaism, a sense of what it is all about, a role Jews are supposed to be playing in the world. Not only *is* there such a core, but I intend here to adduce traditional sources to define at least part of that core in a way that should be indisputable.

I have to argue this because many Jews have stopped believing in any such unifying beliefs. Given the many debates about aspects of the religion and the many subsects of Orthodoxy, it is easy to get used to thinking that Orthodoxy covers a lot of broadly related groups of Jews with no shared fundamental bedrock.[2]

---

2. Indeed, Aviezer Ravitzky has argued just that, in a book titled *Orthodox Judaism: New Perspectives* (Hebrew), eds. Y. Salmon, A. Ravitsky, and A. Ferziger (Magnes Press: Jerusalem, 2006). On the other hand, there are also some who have come up with ideas close to those I offer here, such as Tovah Ilan, in *Minds Across Israel* [Hebrew: מחשבות ישראל, perhaps better translated as *Thoughts of Israel*] (Jewish Agency: Israel, 2003), pp. 70–75, and Gilli Zivan, *Religion Without Illusion — Facing a Post-Modern World, An Inquiry into the Thought of Soloveitchik, Leibowitz, Goldman and Hartman* (Shalom Hartman Institute, Faculty of Law, Bar-Ilan, Hakibbutz Hameuchad: Jerusalem, 2005, pp. 86–87 (Hebrew)). While I do not agree with everything they wrote, the overall picture has much in common; I am particularly taken with Ilan's citation of a Hasidic saying that even the worship of God can become a form of idolatry, and Zivan's note that Orthodox *halachah* has to always build on what came before, not start anew in each generation. The major reason I find myself unable to leave their work without further additions, though, is that they do not prove their contentions; I hope here to prove my view of these issues, showing that at least the ideas in Part One are unequivocal, undebatable, and undeniable.

Let me note here that while I will offer footnotes as I make points that I think need further discussion, and I have tried to do my homework on the topics on which I am writing, I make no claim to have covered the existing literature on these topics fully, nor to have offered a full scholarly accompaniment to the discussion in the text. Similarly, I have chosen to transliterate Hebrew words in a popularly recognizable

Others who share my certainty misidentify the religion's core; for one easy example, many Orthodox Jews equate their religiosity with "keeping *Shulchan Aruch*"; that statement ignores the fact that many areas of that Code of Jewish Law do not apply to all Jews. Further, there are important elements of Jewish religiosity that did not find their way into the Code, as the *Mishnah Berurah* noted over a hundred years ago.[3]

The Essence as a Rubric for Setting Priorities

Another flaw in defining Judaism as the observance of *Shulchan Aruch* or keeping Torah and *mitzvot* is that the size of those corpuses — there are four parts and thousands of chapters to *Shulchan Aruch*, thousands of pages of Talmud, and 280 *mitzvot* that apply in the course of an ordinary life even in the absence of a Temple and/or residence in the Holy Land; as *Iyov* (11:9) says, the Torah is "longer than the earth in measure, broader than the sea" — means few of us can honestly expect to keep all parts of the Torah with equal fidelity, alacrity, or enthusiasm.

That is not a problem if the Torah is a random grouping of commandments, with no overall structure, goal, or purpose. If there *is* an overall character or goal to the religion, however, blindly trying to keep all of *Shulchan Aruch* engenders the possibility of missing the forest for the trees. Two people, each with the time and spiritual energy to fulfill *x* commandments, might differ widely in their religious excellence, one lucking into the laws that are central to the religion's concerns and the other, through no fault of his or her own, hitting only laws meant as secondary. Avoiding that, helping us all see where to most productively invest our time and energy, is one of my central goals here.

---

way, although citations of academic literature reproduce the spellings they use.

3. 156:4.

The Way I'm Going to Do It

I spend the first part of this book, therefore, laying out the most fundamental, irreducible parts of Judaism. Let me stress here, and I hope you will keep this in mind throughout this first part, that I am *not* trying to convince you of what I *personally* think Judaism ought to be; I am trying to share what is *unequivocally* the core of what God (and our Sages) tells us what Judaism was intended to be. That means I will omit many important values, ideals, and practices, not because I personally am unaware of their relevance or importance, but simply because, for whatever reason, they are not as unarguably central to the religion as those I will discuss.

Torah and *mitzvot* communicate that core, mission, or essence in its broadest terms, but do not completely or even sufficiently capture it. In the second part of this book — The Necessity of Autonomy — I aim to prove (and that section will include some personal readings of texts; arguable, but I hope convincing) that God never wanted our religiosity to be fully defined by specific commands.

In fact, I argue that traditional sources show humanity repeatedly and steadily failing to live up to the challenge God set us, to use our human freedom to articulate our own reasonable picture of what it means to serve God. And yet, even with our many prior failures, I can show that Torah and *mitzvot*, as detailed as the system seems to be, still leave us with more autonomy than we recognize, and that our use of that independence is the true marker of how successful we are at building a relationship with God.

If my ideas were theoretical or academic, I might leave this book in my laptop. My interest in spreading it stems from my belief that taking these ideas would point us in the direction of seriously needed change, for Jews, Judaism, and the world. Another way to think of this book, then, is as support for my claim that we need to greatly recalibrate our religious efforts, as individuals and as communities. At several stages of the discussion, but especially in the conclusion, I will stop to consider how different the world would be if these ideas were to get the play and place they deserve.

Let me close this introduction with a brief word about how I have put it together. I want reading this to be as easy and enjoyable as possible, while still discussing ideas in a reasonably sophisticated way. To that end, I have worked to limit the number and length of the footnotes containing extraneous discussions.

I also strive to keep chapters short, so that no piece of the book becomes a burden; I know well the feeling of flipping pages, looking for the end of the chapter so I can put a book down for a bit. Much as I hope you'll want to read it start to finish the first time you pick it up, I am more concerned that the reading, in however many snippets or sessions, be a voyage of pleasurable discovery, as the research has been for me.

On that research: I have come to these ideas over long years of finding the same themes cropping up while looking into ostensibly unrelated topics. Periodically, I would write down some of these ideas, only to realize the picture was not yet strong enough or compelling enough to deserve full-length treatment. At this point, I hope and believe that what I have to say is developed and useful enough to merit your time and attention. And I hope after you finish, you will agree.

That's it, then; to the thing itself.

Chapter 1

How to Find Unarguable Sources
for a Mission of Orthodox Judaism

There are all sorts of reasons to deny the possibility of what I have set out to do, and in other places I have tried to deal with them.[1] The most convincing rebuttal, however, is simply to do it, to get started on finding sources that demonstrate an indispensable and unarguable core to Judaism.

Yet there is one piece of introduction I cannot avoid: my desire to be incontrovertible means I have to first talk about kinds of proofs I consider unarguable. Most obviously, it means I cannot base any of my claims on a personal interpretation of texts. When I read a verse or story from the Talmud, I cannot assume that just because the source's meaning and ramifications are obvious to *me*, that that is the only way to read or understand it.

There is no foolproof way around this problem, and in parts of the second half of this book, I will abandon the attempt and offer precisely such personal arguments. In this first half, though, I have worked mightily to identify sources whose simple and obvious meaning, commonly accepted by hundreds or thousands of years of Jews, support my argument. In line with that, I will often have to avoid giving details of a particular idea, since the details are irreducibly debatable.

Of course, you can't make everyone happy, and some people are so set in their ways that they reject what ninety percent of people would call the simple reading of a text. For one example, a reader of an early draft of this book objected to my translating נפשך as "your soul," since, he thought, the intent of that word in

---

1.　See my Mission of Orthodoxy posts at blog.webyeshiva.org, posts 1–4.

Biblical times differed from how we understand it now. I grant I cannot avoid interpretation to that extent, but am doing my best.

Be Not Overquick to See the Central

The second concern is finding texts that characterize the tradition as a whole. One quick kind of source, which might seem the most obvious place to look, is when the Talmud and Midrash make a statement that encapsulates Judaism in seductively pithy ways, stating that some matter is the "whole" of the religion or the like. By studying a classic and much-quoted example, I can show why those will not be useful here.

The Talmud tells of Hillel being approached by a potential convert who had already been rebuffed by Shammai; the convert wanted Hillel to teach him the entire Torah while standing on one foot.[2] Hillel answers, "What is hateful to you do not do unto others, that is the whole Torah; the rest is commentary, go and study."

Many take this as proof of Judaism's central focus on interpersonal ethics. I am all in favor of improving our ethics; indeed, ethics will turn out to be vitally important to the core I find as well, but this text cannot prove that. Rashi (generally the Talmudic interpreter of original resort) offers two interpretations of the word לחברך, to your friend, and the first sees it as referring to God. In that case, Hillel's essence of Judaism consists of avoiding that which was hated in the eyes of God, without any interpersonal element implied.

---

2. *Shabbat* 31a. This is the standard translation; Dr. Elka Weber told me of Mordechai M. Kaplan's idea that the word רגל might build off the word *regula*, or rule, in which case the convert sought a central rule for Judaism. Prof. Menachem Kellner gave me the reference for R. Jospe's fuller discussion in "Hillel's Rule," *Jewish Philosophy: Foundations and Extensions*, vol. 1 (Lanham: University Press of America, 2008), pp. 191–204.

What Kind of Ethics Did Hillel Mean?

Rashi does offer the more literal explanation that Hillel was speaking about how we treat human friends, but even that does not yet make this a viable candidate for a core of Judaism, despite its own apparent claims to be so.

Look, for example, at the statement's phrasing. While many quote the rule as "Do unto others as you would have them do unto you," Hillel spoke in the passive, telling his convert to *refrain* from mistreating others, not how to act towards them. I think those who stress the ethical in Judaism intend a religion of active kindnesses to the poor, the hungry, and the ill, which is perhaps why it has become so common to restate Hillel's idea in the active. That is fine, but it is not what Hillel called "the whole Torah."[3]

Many also assume Hillel referred to an intuitive ethics, perhaps because he speaks of "what is hateful to your friend," as if the friend determines what is right or wrong. But the last part of Hillel's sentence, "the rest is commentary, go and study," points to Torah and its laws as the place to find the information that expands his rule. If so, even if Hillel intended to encapsulate all of Judaism in one rule, that rule is an ethic defined by Torah, not an ethic right-thinking people come up with on their own. And, to return to my theme, it would mean we still have to explore if we want to find a core or mission of Orthodoxy that can be translated into practical terms.

Did Even Hillel Mean What He Said?

Going one step further, the context in which the Talmud presents the story suggests Hillel himself did not mean the statement as fully as it sounds. The story is one of three in which Hillel converts a person who had made an outlandish demand as part of

---

3. One might perhaps argue that the negative subsumes the positive, since neglecting to perform active kindnesses is hateful to others, but it leaves us to wonder why Hillel would not say it in the positive.

his request to become Jewish (in contrast to Shammai, who sent the person away).

One of those other potential converts wanted to accept only the Written but not the Oral Law and the other to be guaranteed he could one day be High Priest. Each time, Hillel answered as if he accepted the condition, and then masterfully and successfully guided the convert to proper study and practice. The series closes with the three converts meeting and agreeing that Shammai's rigid approach would have kept them from service of God, whereas Hillel's gentler strategy brought them under the wings of the Divine Presence.

The point of the stories, then, seems to be the contrast of the two sages' approaches to difficult people, not the specific content of Hillel's statements. Shammai, perhaps overly focused on ensuring initial sincerity, chased away people who later became full and fully obedient Jews.

I think it no coincidence that these stories immediately follow the famous one of the man who lost a bet that he could anger Hillel. In all these stories, the focus is on Hillel's character, not his specific words. His approach may have lost sight of truth at the beginning — the conditions laid down by the other two converts were completely unacceptable, as the unfolding incidents show — but more successful in the long run.

Another reason to doubt that Hillel's words represent his philosophy of Judaism is that *Avot*, the tractate of Mishnah that records important rabbis' mottos and sayings, devotes seven paragraphs to Hillel's pronouncements. This one does not appear; whatever Hillel meant, the editor of *Avot* did not see it as central to his thought.

Saying It's Central Doesn't Mean It Is

Hillel's example shows why we cannot take even explicit declarations of an idea's centrality at face value. The Talmudic literature may for rhetorical reasons declare particular *mitzvot* equivalent to the whole Torah (as in *Bava Batra* 9a, regarding charity), state that one who violates a particular *mitzvah* loses his share in the World to Come, or note that the Torah emphasized one *mitzvah* more than other commandments (as in *Nedarim* 31a, regarding circumcision).

Indeed, in an appendix to *You Shall Be Holy*,[4] Rabbi Joseph Telushkin lists "The Nine Most Important Commandments According to the Rabbis," places where the Rabbis refer to a *mitzvah* as "of equal significance with all the other commandments combined." On more careful examination, though, each of those statements might be homiletics or hyperbole. An easy example is *tsitsit*, the obligation for men to place strings as fringes on four-cornered garments. While the Talmud describes it as the equivalent of the other commandments, there is in fact no obligation to wear such a garment. Were *tsitsit* truly so central, would we not expect such an obligation?

I will therefore not use such statements; it seems to me they are too open to selective quotation and are also convincing only to those already prone to agree with that perspective. As I stubbornly seek unequivocality, sources that clearly determine the religion's essence, I will look elsewhere.

I build instead from the simplest readings of texts from Scripture, the Talmud, and theological or *halachic* claims that have been accepted by virtually all traditional thinkers. To avoid even unwitting subjectivity, I also build my argument from several *types* of sources, in the hopes that any holes or flaws in one presentation will be filled in by others. Finding a certain idea centrally in an array of texts, laws, or practices is, I hope, more convincing as proof that it belongs among our core commitments than if that same idea figures in only one set.

I first note sections of the Torah that the Torah itself insisted Jews keep in mind all the time. Given a group of ideas or rituals, those that are present more often seem to me to be clearly more

---

4. Pp. 521ff. He also includes Midrashic statements as much as Talmudic ones, when those are even more likely to be homiletical and/or hyperbolic rather than literal assessments of a *mitzvah's* role.

central than others. Or, in a phrase I heard from a prominent educator, Mary T. Grasso, "behavior is belief." In what the Torah told us to always keep in our consciousness, we will find that which most directly shapes how a Jew approaches the world.

Chapter 2

Keeping the Exodus in Mind, All the Days of Our Lives

This and the following chapters discuss the various imperatives of memory the Torah gives the Jewish people, the Exodus from Egypt, the Giving of the Torah at Sinai, the Song of Haazinu, and the first two paragraphs of Shema. Since we are what we do and say, since behavior is belief, the repeated and constant focus on these ideas identifies them as formative of the Jewish psyche. It is no surprise, then, that they outline a minimal Orthodox theology. This minimal worldview will figure prominently in all the further sources we will discuss but is only clarified by taking up each one in turn.

All the Days of Your Lives: Remembering the Exodus

Devarim (Deuteronomy) 16:3 tells us that the annual observance of the Paschal sacrifice, with the attendant weeklong abstention from leavened bread, was ordained to insure that Jews remember "the day of your leaving Egypt all the days of your life." From here, Rabbinic tradition understood that the Torah obligated a verbal recounting of the bare facts of the Exodus morning and night.[1]

I recognize that *halachah* limited this obligation to men; women are welcome to articulate memory of the Exodus, but not required to. That does not exclude them, however, from the verse's hope that the Paschal celebration would stimulate daily memory throughout the year. Men are obligated to have that memory take

---

1. *Mishnah Berachot* 1:5.

a certain form, but that does not exempt women from the desired impact of the sacrifice.[2]

How God Made a Mockery of the Egyptians

The memory of the Exodus might be the minimal idea that God took the Jews out of Egypt, but *Shemot* (Exodus) 10:2 expands its purview. God explains to Moses that He has allowed Pharaoh to resist releasing the Jews in order to extend the process, to allow time for more and greater miracles. Those miracles, the next verse tells us, are intended so that Jews throughout history will tell their children and grandchildren how God toyed with the Egyptians, specifying the various signs of power God placed upon them.

Strikingly, this is one of only two cases where Scripture speaks of telling grandchildren in addition to children (the other is the story of the events at Mount Sinai, as we will see in the next chapter). God tells us the Exodus occurred as it did at least partially to create a lasting memory of God's might and intercession on our behalf in visible and identifiable ways, a memory we are to pass down throughout our generations.

Were we to stop here, we would already have much that is supposed to characterize a daily Jewish worldview. The requirement to remember the Exodus all the days of our lives forces Jews to repeatedly imbibe basic assumptions such as: there is a God; that God is at least sometimes actively involved in history; God developed a special and lasting relationship with the Jewish people (with responsibilities on both sides) through the experience of the Exodus; and God can, at least sometimes, radically change the course of Nature in ways miraculous beyond our comprehension.

---

2. I believe this model — that men are obligated in certain practices, while women only have to absorb the fundamental ideas or consciousnesses underlying them — explains many of the gender distinctions in religious obligation, as I hope to show later in this book. Here, I just note that the difference the verse creates is only in whether one is required to *recite* the memory of the *Shemot* or just *remember* the event.

The Jew, at the very least, is required to take for granted an understanding of how the world works that is often countercultural and needs to cling to that worldview in the face of whatever pressure arises to change it. Clinging to a worldview means not only formally reciting it as part of a liturgy, but making that assertion part of that Jew's experience of the world, letting it shape as many areas of his or her life as possible.

Repeatedly reminding ourselves of these events should make them foundational truths in our Jewish lives, the warp and weft of how we experience the world. To believe something is not to be willing to mark it off on a survey; it is to recognize it as an animating force. I believe in gravity and therefore will not walk off a high ledge unless I have a death wish; my belief in God and the Exodus should, ideally, inform my approach to the world in equally strong ways.

Providence Today: No Simple Matter

Some might argue that the Exodus proves only that God *once* did so, not that God could or might do so again. Aside from the weight of thousands of years of Jewish opinion that miracles are a continuing possibility (or that they repeatedly occur),[3] I also see the Torah's insistence on our remembering these events as showing them to be paradigmatic rather than one-time wonders. The simplest construction of being told to daily recall what God did to the Egyptians is that that memory bears lasting relevance, even if *those* kinds or levels of miracles will not appear in our lifetimes.

I remind readers I am trying to be as minimalist as possible

---

3. Some moderns, particularly academics, claim that Rambam and other rationalists did not believe in miracles. Rambam is always a problem in discussions like this, because much of academe has accepted readings of his writings that traditionalists (and I myself) find untenable. I will in general try to stay away from those pointless arguments, since minds are closed on both sides, and cite Rambam only when his meaning and intent seems most unarguable.

in the name of articulating that which is most demonstrably unequivocal. I might have claimed that the Exodus tells us that God is always involved in the world in some direct way, but that is not proven by the verses in question. We will have cause to consider Providence again when we get to Haazinu and the second paragraph of Shema, but for now I note only that while many Jews will speak of God's Hand in happy contexts — a recovery from ill health, joyous life cycle events, political victories for the Jews — those same Jews might roundly reject the possibility when they find the ramifications distasteful.

A clear and important example is the general rejection, in certain circles, of the possibility that the natural disasters or plagues we experience today could extend from Divine Providence. One reason for that resistance, I fear, is that some contemporary religious thinkers explain events in simplistic, undernuanced ways, blaming others towards whom they are already ill-disposed; this easily gives a bad name to the whole endeavor of identifying God's role in world events.

Given the flaws each of us bear, to point a finger at others' sufferings and ascribe it to the particular sins of which I might be free can come off as smug, not an expression of a relationship with God. That is not the same as empathizing with the suffering of the unfortunate, taking all possible steps to alleviate that suffering, and then suggesting there may be a lesson to learn, not just for those "others," but for ourselves. In any attempt to understand Providence, humility must be central.

More important, though, is that we can and should differentiate believing in Providence as a possibility — which leads believers to be on the *alert* for it, to *wonder* whether particular events are a function of direct divine intervention — from asserting confidently or overbearingly that we know exactly how that Providence is acting and why. If a lesson of the Exodus is that God sometimes ruptures the order of Nature to alter the course of history, there is a value in that lesson independent of whether we can ourselves ever unequivocally identify an instance of its happening or the reason behind it.

Such an approach means that we may individually or in groups come to believe that a certain event is a function of Divine Providence despite our inability to prove it, while others would see God's Hand in different events. It is not the particular insight that is crucial, but the awareness of Providence as a general concept and the interest in seeing if and when it affects the world. The reminders of the Exodus tell us of the *possibility* of Providence, not any particular perspective on when and how that Providence expresses itself (outside of "ordinary" Nature, which is itself always a matter of divine grace).

Remembering the Exodus in Practice

To my mind, a striking example of a person recognizing Providence, an example of faith in action, is R. Yoel Bin-Nun's decision, in the early 1990s, to accept that the State of Israel needed to cede land in the West Bank and Gaza to the Palestinians. Despite being a founder of Gush Emunim, a group dedicated to keeping hold of those territories, he took the longtime Israeli failure to establish firm hold of those lands as a sign of God's Will. Many disagreed with his analysis (and would see later events as proving they were right), but the example of faith pushing him to change long-held political views (at great personal cost) is remarkable and too rare.

The same is true of carrying the Exodus with us. Leaving aside for a moment any of the other messages the Torah gives us, when we are faced with moral dilemmas or with possible outcomes that cause us fear, we are supposed to know that there is a God in the world, that that God runs the world (whatever the mechanism), and that our task is to try to act with the morality God gave us and to expect and hope God will run the world in the way most beneficial to and comfortable for us (even if beneficial and comfortable diverge).

The more we incorporate our experiences and align them with the existence of the God Who took us out of Egypt, the better we are fulfilling this aspect of the religion. There are, of course, exaggerated, silly, or inaccurate ways of doing that, but as a first step in defining the framework of a Jew's life, remembering the Exodus already puts many important pieces in place.

Chapter 3

Guarding Our Souls by
Remembering the Giving of the Torah

The Rabbis of the Mishnah refer to *Shavuot* as עצרת, a term that likely results from their seeing the holiday as finishing up the religious business of *Pesach* (Passover). In perhaps a similar vein, the importance of daily memory of the events that happened on the first Passover leads smoothly into the requirement to keep in mind the Giving of the Torah, commonly connected to *Shavuot*.

The First "Never Forget"

In this case, though, *Devarim* 4:9 does not tell us merely to remember the event — which might have meant, to some, maintaining it in latent memory but not as an active part of one's consciousness — but to "guard yourself and guard your soul well lest you forget the events that your eyes saw and lest they leave your heart all the days of your life, and you shall make them known to your children and grandchildren." The next verse clarifies the reference, making it specifically about the gathering at the foot of Mount Sinai to hear God's words.

The Torah here did not express a *hope* for us to share this information with our children and grandchildren, as in the Exodus, it *required* it. This is the only example I have found of the Torah obligating grandparents regarding their grandchildren. This means that, building only from Scripture, a Jewish approach to the world already must include the continuously remembered knowledge that at least once in history, an entire people experienced direct revelation from God. Forgetting Sinai, Scripture tells us, endangers our souls.

Let me add two caveats to that paragraph. First, as earlier readers reminded me, there is much dispute as to what actually occurred at Mount Sinai. Whatever it was, all agree that the entire people had an experience of revelation that confirmed to them, for all history, both the fact of prophecy and of the special quality of Mosaic prophecy in particular. Second, I make no claim to know the nature of the danger in which we would place our souls by forgetting Sinai, only that the Torah says clearly that we are so doing.

The Loss of a Linchpin of Orthodox Faith

As clear and unequivocal as the Torah's stress is, this knowledge has become untrue for many who otherwise identify themselves as Orthodox. Whether out of ordinary religious doubt or as a function of an intellectual commitment to conclusions reached by science and/or academe, I repeatedly meet Jews — Orthodox Jews — who wonder whether God really exists, whether the Torah is really divine, and how we can know.

As understandable as I find doubt, these questions would take a different shape if more Jews incorporated even just the two pieces of memory I have spoken of so far into their view of the workings of the world. As part of a Jew's *daily* reality, Scripture is telling us, the Jew must keep in mind that he or she is a direct descendant of people who, after being taken out of Egypt by God, *themselves heard and saw* the Revelation at Sinai.

That is an important nuance, since many nations or religions have foundation myths. But the point of Sinai is not that we have a *tradition* that it occurred, it is that our parents tell us what they heard from their parents, in a direct line, back to eyewitnesses.

I find the idea of the Revelation at Sinai as the bedrock of our faith resonant because it was how my father ob"m (of blessed memory) explained it to me when I was a teenager. The loss of faith we find even among many Orthodox people reveals a loss of that central idea, that God spoke to our entire people at Sinai. In an experience I have had more than once, I recently ate with

American students in Israeli *yeshivot*, and one casually mentioned it would be nice if he could have some proof that God exists, that the Torah is divine, etc. I mentioned our direct ancestral tradition attesting to the reality of the event at Sinai, and he and his friends all agreed that while interesting, the claim did not prove the point nearly as well as solid archaeological evidence might.

Again, sympathetic as I am to their struggles, I note that it already shows a failure in the community's transmission of its experience of the world. What the Torah says unequivocally is that knowledge of basic aspects of the world — not amenable to scientific proof — was vouchsafed to us as a people in a series of events at the founding of our nation. We are supposed to continually remember these events, shape our lives in line with those memories, and (I assume but cannot prove) bear witness to them as well.[1]

That we have not succeeded even in maintaining our own awareness of the essential quality of these memories — and our certainty of their basic truth — is only a first example of where Orthodox Jews have lost sight of what Judaism is supposed to be. This can and does translate also into forgetting that the religion's commandments are God given, as we note in the next section.

The Ten Commandments as an Extension of Sinai

The Torah does not specifically apply the requirement to avoid forgetting to the content of the revelation, only the experience. Rabbinic tradition does, as I will show in a moment. As a first step, I suggest that remembering of the Ten Commandments would fit even a simple understanding of what the Torah included in the experience of Sinai we need to never forget. I pause here, then, to review the most unequivocal claims in the Decalogue.

---

1. Ramban, in his commentary on *Shemot* 13:16, specifically gives this as the reason God made the Exodus so remarkably miraculous. Since God is not going to perform a miracle when each new doubter comes along, the legacy of the Exodus was supposed to stand in its place.

If this seems too far an extension for you, please feel free to skip the next few paragraphs; it will not jeopardize my general claims.

Perhaps as some support, I would note Rabbi Joseph B. Soloveitchik ob"m's famous suggestion to justify the custom of standing for the public reading of the Ten Commandments; some worried that this improperly privileges this reading over others. The Rov, as he is known in my circles, argued that this Torah reading *does* differ, not because its content is more important, but because it reenacts Sinaitic revelation. If so, lessons of the Decalogue become a necessary part of not forgetting the event.

The first three of the Ten reiterate the need to believe in the God Who took the Jews out of Egypt, to the exclusion of other powers or idols. The commandment to observe the Sabbath is explicitly connected to remembering both the Exodus and the belief in the creation of the world in six days (literal or not). At the very least, then, the first four statements in the Decalogue ratify and strengthen the nascent theology we have found so far: Jews are a people who believe in a God involved in history, Who took us out of Egypt, and obligates us to follow His commands, ritual or ethical, to the exclusion of worshipping any other power in the world.

A First Stab at Orthodox Ethics, But Not an Unequivocal One

The rest of the obligations, to honor parents, to avoid murder, incest, kidnapping, false testimony, and coveting all carry messages, but my views may stray into personal interpretation. In addition, I am not attempting to extract *all* the significant messages of our texts, only those least amenable to debate.

Many of the ideas I find in the other six commandments will also become clearer in later chapters, the ones that utilize directly *halachic* texts to inform our understanding of Judaism. For example, the prohibition against incest is a first indication of the religion's abhorrence of improper sexuality, but we will see that more convincingly later.

The obligations to honor and fear one's parents are often seen as an expression of gratitude.[2] Yet the central Talmudic discussion of these commandments seems to point instead at the parents' role as co-creators,[3] since it notes the parallels Scripture draws between our attitudes towards our parents and towards God, mentions the tripartite partnership in forming a human being, and, later, records approvingly R. Yosef's reaction to hearing his mother's footsteps, "Let me rise before the Divine Presence that comes." That may also explain why this commandment is among the first five, often seen as articulating obligations between a human being and God.

Accepting that construction of the *mitzvah* — and I grant that it is not as unequivocal as other points I have been making — would deepen our sense of the God focus of the religion, in that even a seemingly intuitive activity such as honoring parents becomes woven into our constant awareness of, and devotion to, God.

The theme of the intuitive being translated into the God-oriented seems to me to characterize the Torah's presentation of murder, kidnapping, and adultery as well. In our times, this is clearer than in the past, since *halachah* defines the first and third of those three in ways at odds with current "intuitive" morality. Many people today — including some Orthodox Jews — would differentiate killing a person who has a chronic or terminal illness, especially if it is painful or the patient gives consent, from murder perpetrated against an ordinarily healthy person. Many more, I suspect, would not see adultery as a capital crime, or even one necessitating the cessation of the betrayed marriage.

I will say more about these when we get to legal or *halachic*

---

2. Reading the first part of *Sefer haChinuch's* reasoning for this *mitzvah*, for example, would give the impression that it was a matter of such gratitude.

3. See *Kiddushin* 30b-31b. The second half of *Sefer haChinuch's* reasoning comes closer to this view, shifting the discussion to how relating to one's parents shapes the person's relationship to God.

sources, but already here we can and should note that the content of the revelational event Jews are warned to never let leave their consciousness articulates a morality many Jews today fail to internalize. The same and more apply to false testimony and covetousness, which are recognized as wrong, but not at a level of Decalogue-seriousness.

Remembering Sinai: Does It Include the Entirety of Torah?

The Talmudic tradition goes further than I have here, taking for granted that the Torah's requirement not to forget Sinai extends to *all* of Torah. *Avot* 3:8 warns against deliberately forgetting any piece of Torah learning, and cites our verse to show that it entails soul-liability. Importantly for our discussion, the Mishnah refers to forgetting any of "משנתו, his Mishnah," which includes the Oral Law in the injunction.

In another initially challenging source, *Kiddushin* 30a discusses a grandfather's obligation to teach Torah to his grandson. It cites the story of Zevulun b. Dan, whose grandfather taught him the entirety of Torah — Written, Oral, and more — and cites our verse as support for the notion that grandfathers have to be involved in the teaching of their grandsons. This again assumes that the study of Torah *in general* is encompassed by the verse's requirement to remember Sinai. In both of these sources, the attestation of verses is offered without debate or suggestion that it is a novel view.

The late R. Moses Feinstein ob"m assumed that the obligation to remember Sinai meant that the obligation of Torah study extended to the entirety of both the Written and the Oral Laws. He made this claim despite the Talmud, in the story of Zevulun b. Dan we just mentioned, limiting the father's minimal obligation to the study of Scripture.[4]

---

4. R. Feinstein, *Iggerot Moshe, Yoreh Deah* 4:36 cites *Menachot* 99b, which quotes Resh Lakish making a similar comment to the Mishnah in *Avot*,

The Talmudic tradition thus seems to show that the Exodus and Sinai are supposed to embed a significant and detailed historical consciousness in the daily lives of the observant Jew, a consciousness with many practical ramifications. Three other texts that we are required to remember often or constantly broaden and deepen the messages of the texts we have already seen, as we discuss in the following chapters.

citing our verse for support. I have written more extensively about the commandment to study Torah in "Choices and Values in the *Mitzvah* of *Talmud Torah*," *Journal of Halakhah and Contemporary Society* XLVII, Spring 2004.

Chapter 4

Haazinu and the Reading of Shema

A Song for Lasting Memory

Haazinu, (Devarim, 32; 1–43) is a remarkable section of the Torah in several ways. First, at least according to some commentators, it was the need to write Haazinu that underlay the commandment for each Jew to write a Torah scroll. Rashi and Rashbam explain the word שירה, song or poem, in *Devarim* 31:19's "ועתה כתבו לכם את השירה הזאת למדה את בני ישראל שימה בפיהם, Therefore, write down this poem and teach it to the people of Israel, put it in their mouths," as a reference only to Haazinu.

Halachically, the Talmud (*Sanhedrin* 21b) cites this verse as the source for the obligation to write a personal Torah scroll, which Rambam codifies as the 18th of his positive commandments. He explains that we are not allowed to write only part of the Torah as an official scroll; for him, then, the verse should be read, "Write an entire Torah, which contains within it this song."

This means that at least Rashi, Rashbam, Rambam, and the author of *Sefer haChinuch* (in Mitzvah 613, where he records Rambam's view) thought God was telling Moshe Rabbenu (Moses, who, in turn, was to tell the Jewish people) to write down Haazinu, to teach it to the Jewish people, and place it in their mouths. It was only because of the prohibition to write partial scrolls that we ended up with a *mitzvah* to write the entire Torah; otherwise, possessing a written copy of Haazinu — and knowing that section well — would have been the basic reminder God wanted.

The definition of placing a song in someone's mouth is not completely clear, but the thrust of the Talmudic discussion seems to see it as requiring knowledge of Haazinu and its messages. In *Eruvin* 54b, R. Akiva reads those words as indicating knowledge beyond basic learning, which was covered by the words למדה את בני ישראל, teach it to the Jewish people; the added clause, for R. Akiva, obligates Moshe to teach it to the point that it is well-ordered in Jews' mouths. Later on the same page, R. Hisda rereads the verse homiletically, with the word שימה, place, changed to סימנה, make signs, to suggest that mnemonic devices are necessary to the study of Torah.

Taking this one step further in a different context, Ramban reads the Biblical term to place something in someone's mouth as referring to teaching it well enough that no part of it is lost in the remembering.[1] That seems to drive the *halachic* understanding of our verse as well, since the requirement to write a Torah scroll was assumed by Rosh, as ratified by Tur and *Shulchan Aruch* in *Yoreh Deah* 270, to mean to have available the means of *learning* Torah, not just a technical requirement to write a Torah scroll. It also explains the custom recorded by Rambam in *Hilchot Tefillah* 7:13 that some Jews recited Haazinu as part of the liturgy every morning.[2]

I cite so many sources because no one asserts the idea that underlies all of them, that Jews are obligated to keep Haazinu in mind all the time. That it is also seen as the explanation for the Jewish people's suffering — a question about which there is much hand-wringing in some circles — seems to me to define its messages as central to how a Jew approaches the world.

I also cite so many texts about Haazinu's importance because of the rarity in my experience of a well-established understanding

---

1. Commentary to *Bamidbar* (Numbers) 23:5, שיגרוס אותם בפיו ולא ישכח ולא יפיל מהם דבר "that he should recite them orally, and not forget or lose any piece of them."

2. I should perhaps note that in one of his published *yahrzeit* lectures, the Rov ob"m assumes that שימה בפיהם actually means reading without understanding. However, he then takes for granted that the phrase two verses later, וענתה השירה הזאת לפניו לעד, and this Song will act as a witness towards them, assumes learning with understanding. And, of course, the Rov applied this idea to all of Torah, in line with what we have seen about Haazinu.

of Haazinu. While most Jews I meet know the basic Exodus and Revelation stories, the content and meaning of Haazinu is esoteric to even fairly educated Jews. Rejuvenating Haazinu's place within the Jewish experience of the world is certainly one contribution I hope to make to the tenor of Jewish thought and conversation, one piece of the crown I hope to restore.

The Message of Haazinu

With that introduction, it should be no surprise that Haazinu echoes ideas we have already seen. The forty-three verses of the Song make too many points to discuss here, but two central ones jump out, from the verse, "זכר ימות עולם, בינו שנות דור ודור, שאל אביך ויגדך, זקניך ויאמרו לך," translated as "Remember the days of old, consider the years of ages past; ask your father and he will inform you, your elders and they will tell you."

Rashi understands the reference to world history to mean we should recognize that God has punished nations in the past (including the Jewish people) for their failures, and that God has the power to bring the Messianic era and the World to Come, should we merit it. Rashbam seems to encapsulate the Song's message as being the recognition that God punishes sinners, the element he emphasizes when explaining the Torah's call to place the Song in the people's mouths.

While I am picking a particular verse and two commentators to support the point, the simple reading of the Song says as much. The first part (until verse 15) speaks of what God did for the Jewish people; taking them out of Egypt, protecting them, and giving them great material bounty. Four verses then outline the Jews' abandoning God, leading to a brief review of the consequences of their so doing, including God's removing protection from them, which leads to suffering. Verse 29 comes back to the theme of our needing to recognize this flow to history, that if only we would be wise, we would understand that the course of our national history ebbs and flows with our faith.

There is more, and a full interpretation of Haazinu, like all of Torah, is certainly worthwhile; but we have, for our purposes, seen enough to show that the central theme of the Song echoes a point we already considered in the context of remembering the Exodus, that the Jewish people live under God's Providence and that at least our national fortunes are intimately connected to our spiritual state. It is a theme that will come up again in just a moment when we get to the recitation of Shema.

Haazinu's having been the source of the *mitzvah* to write Torah scrolls, currently understood to include surrounding oneself with books of Jewish learning, suggests that it, like Sinai, lays out a focus of Torah study. In some extended sense, all Torah learning seems meant to place before our continuing consciousnesses the idea that the history of the Jewish people is based in its relationship with God.

There may seem to be little practical outlet for such a view today; since we have to negotiate our lives in a world populated by those who do not share that perspective, it should still be central at least to Jews' *internal* experience of world events. When the State of Israel experiences continuing drought or other troubles — even as many of its inhabitants have abandoned Torah observance and faith in God — we may need to focus on practical ways to alleviate that suffering, since spiritual solutions on a broad scale are not so forthcoming. But even as we pursue practical avenues, those attuned to the Torah's messages need to also remember the central Jewish belief that a more effective and complete solution would be a spiritual one, a return to a life where we all recognize basic truths about God and history. It is not a matter of effort, it is a matter of internal experience and recognition, and the more we do it, the closer to what God wants of us we get.

Keriat Shema

The final two texts the Torah itself identifies as central to daily Jewish experience are those we say as the first two paragraphs of Shema. In each case, the Torah says Jews must keep "these matters" on their hearts, teach them to their children, and speak about them "when you sit in your house, when you walk on the road, and when you lie down, and when you arise."

Although "these matters" could be taken as referring to all of Torah, tradition narrowed it to the sections of the Torah in which the verses appear. In addition, as a *halachic* matter, there is much debate as to what texts were included in the Torah's obligation of twice-daily recitation. The most extreme position holds that any recitation of Shema is only rabbinically obligated, but the majority position, it seems to me, is that at least the first two paragraphs are biblically ordained.[3]

The first paragraph reminds us of the Jewish belief in a single God (a term we will have cause to discuss again, when working on finding universally accepted Principles of Faith), the undefined (or multiply defined) obligation to love God wholly and completely, and the obligations to place reminders of our connection to God prominently — in our speech, as articles of clothing (the *tefillin*, originally meant to be part of a Jew's regular attire, not a ritual object), and adorning our dwelling places.

VeHaya Im Shamoa — Providence, Reward and Punishment, and the Nature of Nature

The second paragraph speaks of reward and punishment, most explicitly of a direct relationship between national religious observance and material prosperity. At the very least, the verse is clear that within the Land of Israel, material success, particularly rain — still an issue in our advanced scientific times — depends on the Jewish people's relationship with God, their proper fulfillment of the Torah.

I would call this the issue of Divine Providence, except that some rationalists (including, apparently, Rambam in his

---

3. *Minchat Chinuch* 420:1 summarizes the various positions. I have, here and elsewhere, translated בניך as "your children" when it more literally means "your sons" and despite Jewish tradition limiting the obligation of these recitations to men.

Commentary on *Avot*), understand this to mean that God embedded in Nature a connection between rain or drought and Jewish observance with no new Divine input.

The irony of this view to my mind, is that we today refer to it as more rationalist than views that speak openly of God's intervention into nature. I find this odd, since that more rationalist view assumes nature itself responds to religious realities. An Israeli meteorologist, in this view, would have to study weather patterns *and* religious patterns to make accurate forecasts about how the Kinneret will or will not be filled by rain! Perhaps even more challenging, it would mean the laws of nature will not have been fully fleshed out by science until they explain the connection between sin and rain.

According to the text, when the Jews love God and serve God with all their hearts and souls, they can expect prosperity; when they fail to, such as by worshipping other gods, they can expect drought, crop failure, and expulsion. Service of God, or its lack, directly affects the Jews' national fortunes, especially in Israel.

Minimal Scriptural Theology and How It Affects a Jew's Life

I recognize that all of this can strike readers as loose, "*hashkafic*" (a matter of philosophy rather than law) rather than *halachic*, and therefore less obviously obligatory. In a few chapters, I will turn to more *halachic* (more strictly legal) texts, the *mitzvot* the Torah commands, and arrive at similar conclusions. For now, I note that our discussion of biblical verses seems to define an observant Jew as someone who walks around with the constant (or at least continual) consciousness that he or she is a member of a people whom God took out of Egypt, as the first step in a continuing relationship.

The definition of the human side to that partnership is remembering the event of the Giving of the Torah, as well as much of its content, particularly those parts of the Torah that remind us of the connection, at least as a nation, between success at serving God (or failure) and our general success (or failure) in life.

I suspect you, as reader, can flesh out how such a consciousness would change your experience of life, but I think the best way to stimulate your thinking is to note how much this picture differs from what is common in the world at large. Atheism has made a serious comeback in our times; many (perhaps most) leading scientists are atheists, some adamantly so. Even belief has become more of a cultural expression than a declaration of one's understanding of how the world works, such that few leading thinkers or public figures experience world events as related to God and God's picture of our actions.

To assert, not as dogma but as a statement about one's understanding of the world, that the Exodus occurred, that the Torah was given in an act of public revelation at Sinai, and that God rewards and punishes, and that God pays attention to what we do, is to take a stand countercultural even for many religious people, and counterintellectual, at least in the sense the broader world uses the word intellectual.

Were I to stop here, I would have already found simple and unequivocal sources that assert propositions disputed by many who call themselves Orthodox Jews today, yet I have barely begun. As we move forward, we should continue to check our religious "pulse," to see where the contemporary climate may have led us astray from our most basic commitments as Orthodox Jews, and to note how simple it would be to get back to what the sources tell us is the essence of what God seeks from us.

My next step is to show that the Talmud itself also highlighted certain texts as capturing central themes and issues of Judaism. By examining those, and seeing how they correlate to what we have found so far, I will find further support for the necessary part these ideas must play in a lived Jewish experience.

Chapter 5

How Jewish Tradition Understood the Prophets' View of Our Goals

In the past chapters, I reviewed texts the Torah itself identified as central to the lived experience of a Jewish life. I stress that I did not use innovative or idiosyncratic readings of those texts to extract those messages. To support my claim that these ideas are eminent in Jewish sources, this chapter will show that the rest of Scripture, Prophets in particular, reveals a similar set of core ideas shaping a Jewish worldview.

Like the Torah itself — even more so — that corpus is too large to absorb in its entirety; here, the Talmud and Jewish tradition have each provided a way of identifying the essential statements of those texts.

Prophetic Theology, the Talmudic Perspective

A passage at the end of *Makkot* 23b-24a gives us the Talmud's sense of what the Prophets meant to stress as the essential aspect(s) of Judaism. This piece is most famous as the source of the tradition that the Torah contains 613 commandments, a claim that spawned the extensive genre known as ספרי מצוות, books of the commandments.

After breaking down the 613 *mitzvot* into obligations and prohibitions, the Talmud reads verses from later in history as attempts to distill those commandments to more manageable proportions. In the Talmud's rendition, King David reduced the 613 to 11, Yeshayahu to 6, Michah to 3, Yeshayahu (again) to 2, and Habakkuk to 1.

The exact meaning of the Talmudic phrase for what they did

— "בא...והעמידן על, so-and-so came and established them on" — is obscure, but Rashi understood these smaller lists as actual substitutes, a way to fulfill a representative sample of the Torah even if a person failed to keep almost all of its commandments. Once again, we see that the kind of recalibration I am arguing for is not to add to the difficulty of Jewish life; it is, in fact, a way of easing it, letting us feel that we are accomplishing something meaningful even if we continue to fail in all the ordinary human ways.

Writing three hundred years later, R. Nissim, a fourteenth century Jewish thinker known as Ran, explains the passage in what seems to me another way of saying the same thing. For him, the various prophets were identifying those *mitzvot* that would lead most directly to the World to Come. Since the World to Come is the reward for fulfilling the Torah, that these *mitzvot* lead most directly to it suggests they are, for Ran, the core observances, sufficient to qualify a Jew for reward.

If Rashi and Ran are not enough to establish that interpretation of the Talmud (I know of no competing ones), let me note the flow of the discussion itself. When trying to identify a prophet who reduced the commandments to one, the Talmud suggested Amos' call (5:4) to "seek Me and live." R. Nachman b. Yitshak objects that "seek Me" might mean by keeping all the other *mitzvot*. From the objection, accepted as valid and which leads the Talmud to offer an alternative verse, we seem to be looking for statements that say something other than to keep the commandments.

Essential Doesn't Dispense with the Rest

This is not to say the Talmud, Rashi, or Ran thought the Prophets were identifying pathways to religious success despite willful violation of the other commandments. Few of the lists mention murder explicitly, for example, yet it is hard to imagine the Talmud could mean that a murderer could adhere to one of these shortened lists and qualify as a valid servant of God. The advantage is only that the person who actively and punctiliously seeks to fulfill these eleven, six, or one will have a whole and meaningful religiosity, without needing to constantly consult a longer list of *mitzvot*.

Elaborating on all the lists would be lengthy, sometimes redundant, and necessarily interpretive, so I will restrict myself to the last three entries for insight into what the Talmud understood to be the Prophets' vision of indispensable observance.

Justice, Charity, and Privacy

At the point where the discussion turns to a prophet who captured all of the *mitzvot* in three dicta, the Talmud cites *Michah* 6:8: "הגיד לך אדם מה טוב ומה ה' דורש ממך כי אם עשות משפט ואהבת חסד והצנע לכת עם אלוקיך, He has showed you, man, what is good and what God requires of you, to do justly, love mercy, and walk humbly with your God."

The Talmud interprets the first two of the three as justice and acts of kindness, and the third as a preference for privacy over publicity. The Talmud pungently clarifies what it means by a preference for privacy over publicity by saying that it primarily refers to weddings and funerals, events ordinarily carried off with great publicity and attention-seeking; as the Talmud notes, if Jews are supposed to prefer modesty in *those* events, all the more so for others.

Taken together, the prophet seems to be telling us that a baseline relationship with God involves justice, kindness, and a sense of proper modesty, an avoidance of showiness or thrusting oneself into the public eye. It is not clear, though, that each of these terms is understood today in the ways the prophet meant them.

First, although many speak of justice and kindness as characteristic of Jewish experience, Michah refers to what God wants from us, making it plausible that justice and kindness are only truly just and kind when we define them as God would, which would mean the *halachic* definition (not always the intuitive one). Much as Hillel told his convert to go and study to fully understand what it means not to do unto others, justice and kindness are concepts that involve study and *then* intuition, as I argue in the second part of this book, not intuition alone.

Even so, *halachic* justice and charity are arguably close enough to the intuitive version that we might not always notice the divergence. The same is not true for "walking humbly with God," if we take it to mean avoiding the public eye. In today's world, even the Orthodox world, this value is turned on its head, where living in the public eye is the only way to validate oneself.

This is a topic that deserves further discussion, since it is one of the central elements of a relationship with God in the Talmud's understanding of Michah, but it necessarily involves personal interpretation of these norms. Instead, I will leave that for another time and move on with the Talmudic discussion so that we can see the common denominators among the definitions offered.

The two-*mitzvot* encapsulation refers only to observing justice and acting charitably. Here again, the verse begins כה אמר ה׳, Thus says the Lord, reminding us that the definitions of justice and charity come from God.

What Kind of Ethics over Ritual?

The paucity of ritual law in these verses is worth noting, as is their focus on interpersonal behavior and acting justly, charitably, and kindly within the context of a relationship with God. Given that the Talmud sees the prophets cited later in its list as refining the earlier vision into ever-smaller groupings, not supplanting them, Habakkuk's claim that the righteous shall live by faith (2:4) would seem to also assume a faith that leads to the kinds of just, charitable, and kind actions referred to above.

If so, this section of the Talmud understands the Prophetic legacy as urging a faith in God that centers on acting justly, charitably, and kindly. This might seem tautological, but for two facts: first, the morality being called for must originate in and be defined by God (a problem for those of us so certain of our insight that we know what can and cannot be considered moral); and second, that many religious people, including but not limited to

Jews, come to ritualize and value religiosity separate from their morality.

Many of these people are in fact moral in their personal lives, some are not; even the moral ones lose the satisfaction of realizing they are serving God when they act in that way. I wonder, for example, how many Jews see their conscientious efforts at their careers, whether in medicine, law, business, or education, as central opportunities — perhaps *the* central opportunities — for expression of their fidelity to God.

Would a lawyer who refrains from dubious billing practices understand that he or she does so as an extension of his or her relationship with God, or as an expression of a basic human commitment to honesty? Would a doctor who heals the sick see that as a privileged opportunity to extend kindness as God does, or, again, an ordinary if laudable human activity?

I suspect that many dismiss those as appropriate but not really religious, certainly not as "religious" as laying *tefillin*, shaking a *lulav*, or hearing the *shofar*. The Prophets' words and the Talmudic interpretation argue for a shift in our definition of "religious," turning what is now the ordinary human into the backbone of what defines a relationship with God. And, as before, articulating that change of perspective to ourselves and to others seems to me a central part of a Jewish life.

The Talmud clearly cherry-picked prophetic verses, so we might choose to strike this passage for having too clear a program. Besides, some have argued to me this text has no *halachic* ramifications and might be an *aggadic* source, of the kind I said we should not use. I would first note that this text *does* have *halachic* ramifications, since it shapes the counting of *mitzvot* throughout Jewish history.

But I can do better than that. By analyzing the texts used for *haftarot*, sections of Prophets read after the Torah reading on Sabbaths, holidays, and other special occasions, we will see that the messages attentive Jews have heard weekly in synagogue have driven home many of these same points for hundreds if not thousands of years.

The *Haftarot* and Their Theology

The *haftarot* are like the Shema, the Exodus, and the Revelation at Sinai in that they come to the attention of ordinary Jews more often than the rest of Scripture. It is not clear when they developed, but *Mishnayot* in *Megillah* already know of some, so it is a fairly ancient practice.

Since these are briefer than Torah readings, and specifically selected from within a larger corpus, we can expect that they have messages of particular interest. Analyzing all of them is too lengthy a process to engage here,[1] but by focusing only on the most prevalent and recurring ideas and themes, we can see these texts' essential message.

To avoid imposing my own vision on the *haftarot* literature, I have chosen to read through the eyes of Prof. Michael Fishbane, whose JPS translation and commentary is one of the few full-length English-language discussions of these texts. Since he wrote for a broad (mostly non-Orthodox) audience and has no theological ax to grind, the themes he identifies as repetitive would seem to be those so obvious and central that they should be agreed upon by all.

Limiting ourselves in this way leaves only a few ideas. Fishbane notes that national redemption figures greatly in the seven *haftarot* read following the Ninth of Av, and it appears in at least four other *haftarot* as well.[2] More central to Fishbane is the focus on historical parallels, that we read the Song that Deborah sings after the defeat of Sisera in conjunction with the Song sung at the Sea, the incident with the Golden Calf is conjoined to Elijah on Mount Carmel, and the Exodus from Egypt (with its Paschal

---

1. I have done so elsewhere, in a book entitled *Educating a People: An Haftarah Companion as a Way of Finding a Theology of Judaism*, available at *www.lookstein.org/resources/haftarot_book.pdf*.
2. See Michael Fishbane, *The JPS Bible Commentary: The Haftarot* (JPS: Philadelphia, 2002) in the discussion of the *haftarot* to *Bereshit*, p. 4; *Lech Lecha*, p. 18; *Vaera*, p. 88; and *Mishpatim*, p. 115.

sacrifice) parallels the first one celebrated in Canaan, for just a few examples.

Although he does not make the connection, this concern with historical symmetries as he calls them, fits well another theme he returns to often; Divine Providence. Both on a national and personal level, the *haftarot* speak of God as punishing sinners, forgiving the penitent, and eventually redeeming the people.

In several of those, the *haftarah* makes the crucial point that divine justice is meted out "measure for measure" (as the Talmud itself does several times; e.g., *Sanhedrin* 90a), meaning there is a parallel between the reward or punishment administered and the deeds that merited or incurred it.

To land on the positive side of Providence, the *haftarot* speak of recognizing one's sinfulness (as a people and as individuals) and repenting, with emphasis on the moral as opposed to the ritual, on social justice rather than sacrificial practices. One clear exception is the Sabbath, which, as Professor Fishbane notes, is greatly emphasized and whose desecration is singled out as "one of the reasons for the exile."

In his summary, Fishbane highlights "the strong emphasis… on moral right (even over sacral rite)…that the fate of the nation depends upon the covenant obedience of the people…and that the cycle of sin and punishment may be broken by obedience." On the more positive side, he notes that the prophets also "proclaim a future restoration and utopia…a new spirit and knowledge of the Lord…obedience to God will not be learned but a matter of instinct."

Taken together, these themes match well those we have already noted, and that combine to set up a fundamental agenda for the Jewish people: recognizing a unique and unitary God Who oversees the world, rewards and punishes according to people's actions, awaits obedience and repentance to bring eras of bounty and blessing, intends to eventually produce a restored and revivified Jewish commonwealth, and lays out commandments that lead people in these directions.

The content of those commandments, of course, is found in

the realm of *mitzvot,* and we will soon turn to that world to get a sense of whether and which of those are given more emphasis than others. The final step before doing that, though, is to take on the post-Talmudic perspective of central aspects of faith, known as Principles of Faith, to see what has been accepted by rabbinic scholars throughout history as the defining core and mission of a Jew in his or her approach to the world.

Chapter 6

Principles of Faith

Personally, I feel like I've already proven my point, since Scripture, as understood by the Talmud, gives us such clear guidance on the focus of Judaism. Lest you think I have read those selectively or idiosyncratically, I want to turn to one more rich literary tradition that sought to define the core of the religion, the discussions on Principles of Faith, the most famous of which were the thirteen advanced by Rambam.

Principles of Faith: A Way to Define the Essence of the Religion

Prof. Marc Shapiro has recorded a wealth of sources proving that parts of Rambam's Principles were hotly debated, but the Principles still provide a useful starting point.[1] First, in my personal understanding (some disagree), Rambam offered his Principles for reasons similar to mine, as a way to help the ordinary Jew realize the red lines of maintaining good standing as a Jew, despite whatever sins that Jew may have.

It is for that reason, I believe, that Rambam closes his first presentation of his Principles — in the Introduction to his Commentary on the last chapter of Mishnah *Sanhedrin* — with the following words:

---

1. M. Shapiro, *The Limits of Orthodox Theology: Maimonides' Thirteen Principles Reappraised* (Littman Library: Oxford, 2003). I note that I do not intend to fully discuss his points here, just to give a summary of which of the Principles were, in fact, unequivocally accepted throughout Jewish history. I went into somewhat more depth in my Mission of Orthodoxy project, blog.webyeshiva.org, posts 10–12.

> And when all these foundations are established for a person...he has entered the Jewish people, and it is an obligation to love him and to have compassion on him and [to extend to him] all that God commanded us... in terms of love and brotherhood. Even if he has sinned as much as he could due to his lusts and the conquest of his evil inclination, he will be punished according to the greatness of his rebellion, and he has a share [in the World to Come], and he is among the sinners of Israel.

Rambam seems to be advancing a mechanism by which we can decide when a sinning Jew has gone too far; as long as that Jew has not rejected the underlying theology of Judaism, he or she cannot yet be fully excluded from the community of Israel. Similarly, in the third chapter of his *Laws of Repentance*, where he lists people whose beliefs exclude them from a share in the World to Come, he seems less concerned with the World to Come *per se* than defining those sins that, regardless of whatever else this person has done, sunder a relationship with God and require a different level of repentance than ordinary sin.

If I am correct, the literature on Jewish dogma, perhaps starting before Rambam with Saadya Gaon, aimed at the same goal as I have set myself, identifying beliefs and attitudes that allow a Jew to know the difference between failing to live up to a system's ideals and having strayed so far as to cease being part of the system.

The Unarguable Within the Much-Argued

Regardless of that, Prof. Shapiro's research notes Principles that were universally accepted in whole or in part. Those unequivocal assertions echo many of the notions we have already discussed, adding to the sense that they express the worldview that is supposed to sit most centrally for a Jew in his or her daily life.

Some readers might suggest that just because no one in the past argued against a Principle does not stop us from so doing

— just as earlier rabbis argued certain Principles, perhaps so could we. The flaw is that those who disagreed with Rambam claimed Judaism *never* insisted or believed what he asserted, whereas today many would like to claim Judaism *used* to believe *x* (such as Divine authorship of the Torah), but we *now* know *y* is closer to the truth. *That* kind of argument has no basis in traditional Jewish thought, at least for Principles of Faith.

To demonstrate, I will simply pick out those Principles Prof. Shapiro agreed were universally accepted, and then summarize how they would shape a traditional Jewish life.

First Principles: The Existence and Nature of God

The first principle, as Prof. Shapiro puts it, "declares that God exists, that He is perfect in every way, and that He is the cause of the existence of all things." While some think God can do even more than cause all things — some think God could do the logically impossible, such as creating a rock He can't move — it is at least true that Jews believe in a God able to perform all miracles that are not logically impossible.

Allow me to note a few, to give a sense of what it means to believe in God's power. It would mean that *all* Jewish thinkers before and since Rambam thought Jews had to believe that God could, if He so chose, bring victory to a vastly outnumbered army, prevent a nuclear bomb from detonating even once its chain reaction had been set in motion, bring illness to select groups of people identified as sinners (and/or protection or healing to those who had earned God's favor), and provide untold wealth to a nation seemingly bereft of resources.

There is room to argue about which of these God *would* do, or whether a specific incident does or does not stem from God's intervention, but the *possibility* is well-established, and thus needs to be part of any believing Jew's approach to the world.

The second Principle, also universally accepted, speaks of God's absolute unity. While the definition of unity is debated — so that kabbalists, for example, assumed that their idea of *Sefirot* (ten emanations from God, which can seem to be treated as different "parts" of the Divine), even if they are aspects of God, did not violate the Principle — all thinkers have required Jews to assert it (as does the Shema). Any belief that openly rejects the unity of God inherently strays from the core of the religion.

The third Principle speaks of God's incorporeality and sparked much discussion. What Shapiro himself accepts, however, is that by the twenty-first century, the belief that God has no body has taken full root within traditional circles, and would seem therefore to be essential to any traditional version of Judaism.

Creation of the World and the Worship of God

The Principles we have already seen speak of God Himself, as it were, but the next discuss God's interactions with the world and with people. The fourth Principle asserts God's priority, clearly accepted by all Jewish thinkers, but the definition of priority depends on our view of creation, debated ever since at least the time of Aristotle.

Indeed, even the question of what Rambam believed remains unresolved. In contemporary times, different noted scholars have asserted they knew Rambam's "true" position on creation, and matched it up to a different one of the three well-known positions. That is, some argue that Rambam believed in creation *ex nihilo* (from absolute nothingness, as he most explicitly says), that God shaped eternally existing matter into the universe as we know it (similar to the position of Plato), or adopted the Aristotelian view that the earth has always existed pretty much as it is now.

Especially since Prof. Shapiro shows us noted rabbis who explicitly held the Platonic position, we cannot claim Jewish tradition has unequivocally accepted creation from nothing. An adherent of the Platonic view — the closest to the modern Big Bang theory — can find sources to support that position. The Aristotelian position, which some claim Rambam held, is less relevant because it has been fully discredited in modern scientific thought, and also suffers for seeming to rule out miracles.

The part of the fifth Principle that has been universally accepted is that only God can be worshipped. This might seem obvious, except that "worship" need not mean only bowing down or praying towards. Accepting any force other than God as the ultimate ruling power violates this Principle as well. In that sense, the Principle challenges even many Orthodox Jews today, given their commitment to the truths of science.

For many years and in many areas, science focused on particular phenomena, reactions, or interactions, and described only the observed world, with suggestions for how those observations could be explained. Those observations might be challenging to the regnant expression of the religion but were simple truths that had to be confronted, digested, and understood within the broader religious context.

More and more scientists today, however, claim to provide all-encompassing theories or explanations of the world, notably devoid of any place for God, or claim to be on the verge of such a theory, with its outlines already clear and contradictory to religious belief. *Any* such statements need to raise the hackles of a believing Jew (aside from the fact that they are scientifically irresponsible, but that is part of a different diatribe). For Jews, the belief in God and our commitment to only worship God means we must reject any claim to explain the world independent of God.

Here, too, experience has introduced me to many Jews who have lost sight of this Principle and would therefore need to reconsider what it means to believe in God from a Jewish perspective. A God subservient to the Laws of Nature is not a traditional Jewish One, and those who believe in that God have lost sight of a central part of Jewishness, the obligation to serve as a cadre of believers in the One True God.

The first five Principles thus define God and worship of that God. The next seven take up issues that have more to do with building a religious life in this world than theoretical claims about God.

Prophecy, Especially of Moshe Rabbenu

The sixth and seventh Principles assert the existence of prophecy and state that Moses' prophecy was greater than that achieved by anyone who preceded or followed him. There was much debate about when and how prophecy works, but the bare fact of it is well accepted. We also find debate about Moshe Rabbenu's uniqueness, but that is focused on specific challengers, Ezra, Bilam, and the Messiah. For our purposes, then, we can assert a requirement to believe in the uniqueness of the prophecy that produced the Torah as compared to all other Scriptures we possess.

Reminding ourselves of that belief shows why Jews today should reject much in the modern attitude towards Scripture. With all the debate about whether all of the Torah is the result of Moshe Rabbenu's prophecy, a difficult subject that comes to the fore in the next Principle, the fundamental belief that Scripture represents God's direct communication with a prophet implies an attitude towards those writings and the truths they contain that goes beyond the respect we allot to insightful, nonprophetic writers.

There may be interesting literary themes, development of motifs, or wordplay in Scripture as in other texts, but the Torah is above all else the record of God's communication with Moshe Rabbenu, so that it contains truths *revealed* by God, not the extraordinary insights of that special human being. Comments that limit the Torah to the cultural context in which it was promulgated or speak of Moshe's personal concerns as relevant to the conclusions the Torah reached lose sight of this basic fact. The same is true, appropriately adjusted for the difference between Moshe and all other prophets, of the rest of Scripture.

A Necessary Debate: Torah from Sinai

The next Principle, which is highly controversial, seems to require the belief that every letter of the Torah we currently have was given to Moshe Rabbenu at Sinai. The problem, as Shapiro documents at length, is that numerous authoritative *pre*-Maimonidean sources recognize errors in the transmission of the Torah as well as the possibility that scattered phrases (or as much as the last twelve verses) were not written by Moshe. Some even dispute whether those sources were Divinely inspired.

I stressed that these sources are pre-Maimonidean to remind readers that Rambam, too, knew of them. Shapiro suggests, based on his view of how Rambam handled ideas he thought of as esoteric, that Rambam put forth a principle he knew to be untrue but thought important for the masses.

More plausible to me, since I do not believe Rambam ever knowingly lied, is that he meant a narrower expression of the Principle, such as the one Shapiro cites from the

> late *rosh yeshivah* of Yeshivat Ner Israel, R. Ya'akov Weinberg (1923–99). After mentioning some of the points already made, Weinberg states:
>
> > ...[Rambam] knew very well that these variations existed...the words...`the entire Torah in our possession today'...should be understood in a general sense that the Torah we learn and live by is for all intents and purposes the same Torah that was given to Moshe Rabbenu.[2]

This seems to me not only an accurate expression of Rambam's position, but of the traditional one today. Recognizing and accepting that pieces of Torah have a tortured history, whether in specific letters or words, and that the authorship of some sections is in some dispute, we are still left with the significant claim that the vast bulk of Torah is directly dictated by God.

This again becomes crucial in discussing the Torah's attitudes

---

2. Shapiro, p. 116. I recognize contemporary thinkers who strive to assert one can be Orthodox and yet believe in a Torah not given to Moses, such as Prof. James Kugel's *How I Read the Bible*. I will not here delineate my personal disagreements with his arguments; it suffices to note that he and those like him have, with all good intentions, stepped outside the bounds of how Orthodox Jews approach the Torah.

and values. That God legislated certain laws means that, unless the system itself limits their applicability, those laws were ones the Divine wisdom ordained universal and timeless, and we need to recognize them as such, whether we understand it or not.

The Possibility of Change in the Torah or Its Laws

This ties directly to the ninth Principle, that the Torah will never be changed or abrogated. Without delving into it in detail, I can note that those who did contemplate or accept that the Torah could change put conditions on it that have not yet appeared (a national experience similar to Sinai, where God appears to all, or the Arrival of the Messiah are two such examples).

True, certain laws' applications change depending on era or location, but the Principle did not claim that all Torah law applies at every moment of history, just that the Torah *as a system* applies at all times. Barring other conditions, the Torah's prohibitions and obligations should be seen as stating eternal values of the Jewish people, ordained by an omniscient God.

In this view, questioning the morality of *mitzvot* can only come as part of a search for understanding, not as an expression of doubt of the commandment's basic morality. I note this because many Jews, even prominent Orthodox thinkers, allow themselves to dismiss some Torah law as a cultural artifact of the time when it was given or to assume that its basic morality is problematic.

The question of God's knowledge produced so much debate there is little to be said unequivocally, except perhaps that everyone agrees God knows something about the world. That minimum seems necessary for the issue of reward and punishment, the next Principle, since knowledge is fundamental to recompense or retribution.

Reward and Punishment and the Messiah

In reward and punishment, there is likewise significant and intractable debate, except about the basic proposition that people are, at some point, rewarded for their deeds and punished for their misdeeds, whether in this world or the next. As I noted, this implies some continuing accurate record of our actions; however that relates to the question of God's knowledge.

The next Principle asserts the belief in a future redeemer. Here again, there were debates about the details, whether the redeemer had to be from King Solomon's line, for example, or if that redeemer might be God Himself. Like in the previous two Principles, there is an irreducible mimimum. Goodwill, good faith, and sincerity notwithstanding, any Jew who denies the absolute truth of a future redemption has lost sight of Judaism's insistent assertion of how history will culminate.

Resurrection of the Dead and the Nature of Rambam's Esotericism

The final Principle, resurrection of the dead, generated so much controversy I cannot in fact find even a minimal unequivocal expression of it, despite *Sanhedrin* 90a, which seems to assert the necessity of that belief explicitly. That is not to say I have any personal doubts about it, but I am here only including those beliefs so universal as to be unequivocal, undeniably part of what it means to follow traditional Jewish thought.

This brief review obviously leaves out many important nuances and details, but I believe it accurately captures aspects of the Principles that must figure in any minimal presentation of Jewish belief. It also offers us a chance to step back and see where this part of the journey has taken us, the ideas and perspectives our various sources agree are necessary to a traditional Jewish worldview.

Chapter 7

Summarizing the Core of Jewish Belief

Beliefs as a Lived Experience

As we near the end of the theoretical part of our discussion, let me repeat my understanding that when we speak of beliefs, we mean more than just mouthing a formula. I have heard Jews, for example, speak about whether some course of action is prudent, since it might lead to the annihilation of the Jewish people. If by annihilation the person actually means the total destruction of world Jewry, he or she has lost track of the necessary worldview of a Jew, since we *know* the Redeemer will eventually come.

While, God forbid, large percentages of the Jewish people may be destroyed, as the Holocaust proved, God's guarantee of a restoration of a *halachic* state in Israel should mean an Orthodox Jew can never worry about this happening to the *entirety* of the people. That underlying belief may not always free us from fear — we would also not want to act so as to endanger large segments of Jews — but Jews must always recognize and accept that we know the broad outlines of the ultimate course of history.

So, too, the confusion about the nature of the World to Come complicates any attempt to incorporate it in people's lives, but it at least means that Orthodox Jews must, as an essential part of their worldview, see a future in which accounts are balanced and closed for what has happened in the rest of world history.

That has at least two parts to it: first, the constant awareness that there are no actions without consequences, good or bad; and second, the certainty that death is not the end. While we do not know how it looks and works, part of an Orthodox Jew's core experience of the world is the certainty of an existence beyond death to which we aspire and where we are all promised a place.

Fear of Death and the Faith of a Jew

To put one practical touch to that piece of the discussion, I wonder at the different forms fear of death takes. There are many legitimate Jewish reasons to fear death. *Berachot* 28b tells of R. Yochanan b. Zakkai's deathbed fear, which he explained as fear of God's judgment. Confronting the absolute truth about our various personal failings — as happens when we face our Maker after death — is appropriately fear-inspiring.

From another perspective, the Vilna Gaon is reported to have cried on his deathbed because of the impending loss of the ability to perform *mitzvot*; R. Soloveitchik spoke of Judaism's abhorrence of death in similar terms; as quenching human creativity and closing off our ability to contribute to perfecting God's world.

There are others, but I doubt these rabbis' fears are those felt by ordinary Jews today. I speak only anecdotally, but conversations around issues such as end-of-life care and the emotions those arouse seem to me, often, to occur in the absence of any lived or felt belief in a continued existence beyond death. Many otherwise believing Jews cling to life, in my experience, largely because of their instinctive and visceral worry that death is the absolute end. Once again, as we review ideas that might seem purely theoretical, we see they would, properly absorbed into our consciousnesses, shape our actions in our real lives as Jews and in this case, provide some valuable solace in dark times.

The Principles: A Final Review

Our run-through of the Thirteen Principles of Faith has shown how many of them have remained accepted parts of a necessary Jewish worldview despite the armies of thinkers who critiqued them in the centuries since Rambam released his writings.

Four of those make claims about God, that: (1) God is

omnipotent (although perhaps not able to perform the logically impossible); (2) unitary (a term open to debate); (3) God has no physical body in the ordinary sense of the words; and (4) God is prior to the world, whether chronologically or ontologically.

Beyond the direct God-propositions, we found that Jews believe in prophecy, in the special qualities of Mosaic prophecy with room, according to some, for competitors, although not in a way that affects us today. Moshe's prophecy resulted in the Torah, and Jewish faith obligates us to see the contemporary text of Torah for all intents and purposes the same as the one given to him. Further, barring either another prophetic revelation or direct encounter with God as public as the original; the Arrival of the Messiah, which may bring some *halachic* changes; and/or the workings of the *halachic* process, Torah law remains in full force in perpetuity.

Successful observance of that Torah or failure to do so will, again according to essential beliefs, be recorded and remunerated, and some of that compensation will come in the form of a future redemption/return to a Jewishly organized society with a Temple.

With all the caveats, then, we still find in the Principles a basic worldview accepted by all traditional Jewish thinkers and that therefore characterize a traditional Jew. Not surprisingly, much of that worldview is already included in the texts and ideas we saw before, the ones Scripture and/or Rabbinic tradition singled out for attention.

This means — and I grant it's taken a while to say it, but would you have believed it otherwise? — that Orthodoxy, with all its internal struggles and disputes, takes significant and unequivocal positions about the nature of God, the nature of the Jew's role in the world, the existence of record-keeping and judgment over how well Jews fulfill that role, and the course of human history. The religion expects Jews to keep those ideas consistently and continually in mind by reminding themselves at least twice daily of the Exodus, always remembering the Giving of the Law at Sinai, having the lessons of Haazinu in their mouths, and at least twice daily rehearsing the theological ideas in the first two paragraphs of Shema.

Still and all, I worry readers will dismiss this as theory, irrelevant to practice. To counteract that impression, I take a break from the theoretical approach and turn to the world of *mitzvot*, of commandments, the most identifiable characteristic of a Jew's religious life. Asking the same questions we have been — which of the *mitzvot* are core and mission shaping — I hope to show that what is often thought of as the ritually focused aspect of Judaism exhibits the same God-centeredness we found until this point. In doing so, we will take an important step towards recovering what Judaism was really supposed to mean, what a Jewish life was supposed to keep as its central and predominant focus.

Chapter 8

What Death Penalty Prohibitions Tell Us About the Core of Judaism

S ome of you, I hope, are already convinced; of those who are
not, I suspect my failure to deal with *halachah*, Jewish law,
might be a prime reason. *Halachah* gives an impression of clarity
and exactness that many find more attractive as a way of defining Jewishness than theology. Ideas can be manipulated, argued
about, twisted, but focusing on practices or law frees us of the
messiness.

For such people, a Jewish man who wears a beard and sidelocks, a married Jewish woman who covers all or most of her
hair and wears long skirts or dresses, must be Orthodox; in other
communities, the same reaction prevails towards those who care
about Sabbath observance and dietary laws. And the beauty of
it, for these people, is that I can look for those simple identifying
traits and need not look any further.

I write here to show that that view is wrong even within the
parameters of *halachah* itself. That is, even if we ignore or reject
everything I've written so far and operate only within the world
of *halachah*, I believe I can still take us to a similar place, and still
unequivocally, in ways no one could dispute. The irony is that
these laws get even more specific than we have seen until this
point — still indisputably — and yet stress aspects of the religion
that are rarely emphasized today.

Are *Mitzvot* the Same as *Halachah*?

Some points of introduction: First, I will speak a great deal about
mitzvot, commandments given by the Torah, as being *halachah*,

Jewish law, even when those commandments have not been elaborated in as great detail in later legal discussions as others. I assume, and believe it unequivocally true, that if the Torah lays down a commandment, it is part of Jewish law. While Jewish law has much more to it than the commandments, those are still part of that legal system as well, even those left only loosely defined (I will have more to say about loosely defined commandments in the second part of this book).

I mention this because one of the clearest signs that Orthodoxy has strayed from its foundations is that this connection is not recognized even by some of the most educated Jews. To many, *halachah* is what is found in books of codification, while other *mitzvot* are matters for *hashkafah*, Jewish thought. I know this from personal experience; I once oversaw the implementation of a *halachah* curriculum based on *Sefer haChinuch*, a book that enumerates the commandments in the Torah.

Some of the most vigorous complaints came from teachers for whom these discussions were not really *halachah*. For them, the religion is "really" where there are specific laws, such as blessings, Shabbat, dietary laws, holidays. *Mitzvot* with a less well-known[1] or less exactly defined literature are simply not experienced as *halachah*.

This leads to the misconception that these are matters of ethics, recommended or laudable behavior rather than strict obligation, or that the welter of opinions on how to fulfill them means there are no right and wrong ways to do so. I grant the challenge of ill-defined parameters, but note that this leads many to forget actual *mitzvot*, often to even be ignorant of the obligation. This is all the more problematic when some of those laws are demonstrably

---

1. Although that literature is often abundant to those who know how to look for it. For an example of the application of erudition to *mitzvot* that might seem to lack *halachic* content, see R. Daniel Feldman's *The Right and the Good: Halachah and Human Relations* (Yashar Books, 2005) as well as *Divine Footsteps: Chesed and the Jewish Soul* (Lambda, 2009).

more central to how God intended a Jewish life to be shaped than the ones we include in our regularly lived *halachah*.

Looking For the Core of *Mitzvot*

As earlier, I would not want my search for identifiably central *mitzvot* to give the impression that I devalue or undervalue the rest. All human beings are obligated to keep those of God's commandments that apply to them with as much dedication and alacrity as possible, regardless of the source. My search here is only to ensure that our limitations of attention and memory do not lead us to focus on the wrong subset of *mitzvot*. The *mitzvot* I identify here do not define a *good* Jew, since goodness stems from maximal effort; rather, they set the minimum of what defines being part of the system at all.

Also as earlier, I need a method to convincingly identify *mitzvot* that are more central to the religion.[2] A starting point comes by remembering that as soon as the Talmud mentions there are 613 *mitzvot* in the Torah, it immediately adds that 365 are prohibitions and 248 are commandments,[3] so that the marker of importance in prohibitions might differ from that of obligations. Since the line between merely important and core-defining is clearer with prohibitions, I will begin there.

---

2. Aviezer Ravitzky, in his contribution to *Minds Across Israel*, above note 2 in the Introduction, suggested that the foundations of Judaism lie in the three commandments for which a Jew is required to die rather than transgress. The overriding importance of those *mitzvot* is, indeed, clear, but only when an outside actor or force is attempting to coerce the abandonment of Jewish values. I am here interested in the vital and mission-forming aspects of an ordinarily lived Torah lifestyle, some of which God might temporarily forego to save a Jewish life. For an easy example, Sabbath observance is not one of those three, so that in many cases a Jew would be allowed to violate the Sabbath to save his or her life (or someone else's). Yet being Sabbath observant is indubitably part of the mission of Judaism, as we have seen, since it was mentioned in the Decalogue, and as we will see here in the more *halachic* section.
3. *Makkot* 23b.

The Chief Prohibitions: Capital and *Karet* Crimes

For all that Jews are obligated to observe all commandments with equal dedication, the different severity of punishment given to different sins still reflects something about the severity of those sins. I find it interesting that Rambam chose to stress this idea specifically when *Avot* 2:1 spoke of the equal importance of all *mitzvot*. Without subverting the Mishnah's lesson that we should dedicate ourselves to all parts of *halachah*, Rambam reminded us of the realities of the *halachic* system, in which indeed some sins have more of an impact than others. At the top of that list are transgressions that, if committed in the most extreme fashion, would bring either the death penalty or *karet*, excision.

It is always sad to contemplate the possibility of a human court, or God, punishing someone by taking that person's life. To make sure we do not get the wrong impression — I once had a conversation with a teen in which I would periodically ask how Judaism reacts to particular sins, and he consistently (and wrongly) said, "we kill him" — I pause to point out that the detailed technicalities of meting out the death penalty make it hard to imagine that the goal of these punishments was to administer them.

Indeed, a *mishnah* in *Makkot* (1:10) famously commented that a court that administers capital punishment once every seven (or seventy) years is too quick to cause injury. For *karet,* tradition assumed courts could administer lashes as atonement, allowing the sinner to escape with a less severe punishment than justice would have deemed necessary.

However that translated into social governance,[4] the fact of it being so suggests that the value of these punishments lies at least as much in their rhetoric, the message they send about the severity of sins, as in their being put into practice. The Torah categorized some sins as incurring death or *karet* liability, I am

---

4. A question Ran, the 14th century thinker, took up in his *Derashot*, but not our issue here.

suggesting, at least partially or mostly to let us know that these were, in fact, more serious than others.

The Difficulties of Atonement for These Most Serious Sins

Support for that claim comes from the חילוקי כפרה, the different kinds of atonement required for various transgressions, advanced by *Yoma* 86a. There, the Talmud tells us that those who have failed to observe a positive commandment need only repent, those who have transgressed an "ordinary" prohibition need repentance and the experience of Yom Kippur, while those who violate a death penalty or *karet* prohibition need those plus יסורים, suffering. The longer process and the insistence on suffering to achieve full expiation again suggest we are dealing with more severe transgressions.

In addition, these transgressions lessen or sever the sinner's ties to Jewish society in at least two ways. First, simply, these are sins that necessitate literally removing the sinner from society, either by death or God-administered *karet*. Israel's tent is large enough to incorporate thieves, talebearers, and other terrible sinners, probably because we are all sinners. The death penalty or *karet* sins, though, require the sinner's removal, in the biblical phrase, to "cut that soul off from its nation."[5]

The Yom Kippur service performed in the Temple ratifies that view. *Shevuot* 12b tells us about the expiation provided by the שעיר לעזאזל, the scapegoat sent out to the desert, which secured atonement for all Jews. The Talmud notes that the service effectuates spiritual repair even without sinners' penitence, a surprising claim of its own.

More to our point, the Talmud says those whose sins were among the חמורות, the severe ones, which at least includes those that incur the death penalty or excision,[6] *would* have to repent

---

5. As in *Bereshit* 17:14 and numerous other places.
6. Rambam limits it to these, see *Hilchot Teshuvah* 1:2; Kessef Mishneh

to be included. Being excluded from the national sacrifice seems at least a promising way to identify sins that rise to some more significant level of importance to Jewish faith and practice.[7]

All of this seems to me to show that capital and *karet* crimes are one avenue to see the core interests of the religion. I will go through them here, using the list from the eighth-century *Halachot Gedolot* for its convenience (and because there is little significant debate about it), looking for the overall patterns that could tell us what the religion found most deeply problematic in possible Jewish behavior.

Acts That Could, At Their Worst, Deserve Death by Stoning

Behag (acronym for *Baal Halachot Gedolot*, the author of the work *Halachot Gedolot*) notes eighteen commandments punishable by stoning, were the sinner to fulfill all the technical requirements for that punishment. Several of those are sexual, so let me comment ahead of the discussion that the Torah not only prohibits certain types of intercourse, but also "coming close" to such relationships, although "coming close" would not incur the death penalty. The definition of "coming close" is not unequivocal; I mention it to point out that the Torah is deeply opposed to

---

thinks it is possible that the category includes even more transgressions, but takes for granted that these should be included.

7. I concede some saw other sins as more serious than these. *Minchat Chinuch*, for example, several times assumes that a repeated transgression, such as eating several pieces of forbidden meat, might be more severe than a one-time occurrence, such as killing an animal. He bases this on a comment of Ran in *Yoma*, where the question was how to procure food on Shabbat or Yom Kippur for someone ill who needed meat. The Mishnah allows killing an animal (a violation) instead of eating meat that has not been properly slaughtered. *Minchat Chinuch* also assumes that rabbinic commandments are more severe than Biblical ones. In each case, I believe his technical discussion, right or wrong, does not affect my points here, since the severity of *these* sins is not lessened by others being even more serious.

any such inappropriate sexual activity. It is only that some such activity is *so* serious as to lead to a person's death, while lesser such activity is merely reprehensible.[8]

Stoning Prohibitions

Of the eighteen stoning prohibitions, the first six prohibit sexual intercourse with one's mother, father's wife, daughter-in-law, another man, and an animal (Behag has separate prohibitions for a man and a woman in this last category). The next five focus on serious abandonments of God, such as through blasphemy, idolatry, and witchcraft. The twelfth stoning sin is desecrating the Sabbath, then comes cursing a parent, having intercourse with a girl between the ages of 12 and 12½ who has been betrothed to another, attempting to lure individuals or a group to idol worship (regardless of success), being a witch, and being a rebellious son.

An argument can be made that the witchcraft prohibitions are extensions of idolatry, and that the parent-focused sins are also extensions of how we act towards God, since *Sanhedrin* 50a notes that the Scriptural parallel in language for the honor we owe parents and the honor we owe God means to relate the two. If so, the entire list consists of sins either of wrongful sexuality or of mishandling our relationship with God, which, as we will see, is true of a sizable portion of these sins.

The Rest of the Death Penalty Prohibitions

An additional nine sins are punishable by burning, all of them sexual — a man having intercourse with a woman and her daughter, his own daughter, his granddaughter (whether born

---

8. The *halachic* notion of אביזרייהו, extensions of sins, mentioned in *Sanhedrin* 74b, tells us that while we might not administer the death penalty for lesser versions of these sins, they might still be worth dying for rather than transgressing. That, too, suggests these areas are mission-destroying in even lesser versions.

to his son or daughter), his wife's daughter and granddaughter, his mother-in-law, his wife's grandmother on either side, and a priest's daughter who commits adultery. The male partner in that last case would receive the ordinary punishment for adultery, strangulation.

Only two commandments lead to death by the sword: murder and committing idol worship as part of a city where the majority has similarly worshipped.

Strangulation is the lowest form of the death penalty, and the sins that incur that punishment are perhaps therefore something of a catchall: hitting a parent (perhaps still an extension of how we act towards God, as above), kidnapping (perhaps an extension of murder), a qualified elder contravening a ruling of the Great Court, being a false prophet, prophesying in the name of an idol, and engaging in an adulterous affair.[9]

Excision

A further seven sexual sins incur excision, or *karet*, such as having intercourse with a sister, aunt, wife's sister, brother's wife, uncle's wife, or a menstruating woman. Several eating sins incur *karet*, such as prohibited fats and blood (those might be because of their use in the Temple service), leavened bread on Passover, eating or performing prohibited actions on Yom Kippur, leftover or certain improperly offered sacrifices, known as פיגול,[10] and a ritually impure person eating sacrificial meat. Staying with the Temple,

---

9. A similar complication of deciding what to include in the 613 bedevils Behag's no. 38, witnesses who falsely testify against a priest's daughter. This would seem a detail of the prohibition of עדים זוממין, false witnesses who receive the punishment they attempted to impose on their victim. Behag apparently counts it because they receive a different punishment than the intended victim would have received had they succeeded. Either way, they receive the death penalty. A man who has adulterous intercourse with a priest's daughter also appears separately in Behag's list for his differing death penalty.

10. The offering priest assumes, during one of the crucial aspects of offering

we also find *karet* for entering while ritually impure, slaughtering and offering sacrifices outside the Temple, making or anointing oneself with ritual oil, making the ritual incense for non-Temple purposes, and failing to offer a Paschal sacrifice. Last, failure to circumcise oneself also incurs *karet*.

Any one of these transgressions, committed willfully, suffices to exclude a person from the nation, which suggests that we should be able to explain each one's essential importance to Jewish observance. Both for the sake of brevity and because those kinds of analyses are rarely so convincing as to be unequivocal, I restrict myself to noting prominent patterns.

The Importance of Sexuality

Twenty-six of the sins — fewer for Rambam, but not significantly — deal with prohibited sexuality. In today's environment, this bears repeating and emphasizing: of all the prohibitions in Judaism that incur either the death penalty or excision, forty percent stem from illicit sexuality. This would seem to mean that Jews, at the core of the religion to which they adhere, bear witness to God's view of appropriate sexuality as the base standard for the human condition.

In stressing that, I note that Judaism has a view of wrongful sexuality for non-Jews as well, although it is defined slightly differently. It does mean that part of being Jewish is to adhere to and believe in a universal ethic about sexuality, one at great odds with common assumptions of contemporary Western thought.

I recognize that the phrasing is not only out of sync with Western culture, but with much of the Orthodox Jewish world today. Perhaps because of a laudable desire to sympathize with sinners and help them find their way back to God, the past century and a half has seen a revolution in Orthodox responses to deviations from observance generally. In the last decades, as Western

---

the sacrifice, that the sacrifice will be eaten after its right time, invalidating the sacrifice.

society's sexual ethic has changed, there has been a similar move to also be more sensitive to the great pressures and struggles faced by people challenged by frowned-upon sexual urges.

That reaction, it seems to me, true and appropriate in the individual case, cannot be allowed to affect our recognition of how centrally abhorrent these sins are to the Jewish view of the world. In *all* cases of wrongful sexuality — adultery, incest, a woman who is menstruating, homosexuality, bestiality — our practical approach to specific sinners raises different questions than our communal policies and attitudes. In the latter, the religion is clear about striving for what should be, difficult as it is to get there.

Summing Up the Rest

A further eleven of the prohibitions have to do with the Temple and its service. Some of those still apply today, such as not slaughtering or offering sacrifices outside the Temple, but it is an area we can mostly leave for another time. It does show the centrality of proper treatment of the Temple in a full Jewish experience and should reinforce our awareness of how inherently lacking we are in our ability to fulfill the basic religion in the absence of a standing Temple.

Ten commandments legislate issues of idolatry or witchcraft, reminding us of the religion's concern with focusing worship solely on God, on not turning to other powers for assistance or protection. Finally, five sins on the list focus on the most significant holidays of the year, the Sabbath (captured in one prohibition, although one with 39 parts, the prohibited creative labors of the day, the willful commission of any of which suffices to incur the death penalty), Yom Kippur (the prohibitions on creative activity and eating), and Passover (the obligation to bring the sacrifice and the prohibition against eating חמץ, leavened bread).

Sum total, eighty percent of these significant sins focus on sexuality, the Temple, idolatry, or three central holidays. Those holidays have a strong theological component, Sabbath being explicitly a reminder both of the Exodus and Creation, Passover of the Exodus as the foundation of the Jewish people's relationship with God, and Yom Kippur as a day of atonement, a reminder of judgment, Providence, and reward and punishment.

Were this our only evidence, we would come to similar conclusions as we did on theoretical grounds, that Judaism focuses on helping us build a relationship with only God as ruler of the universe, to the exclusion of any other candidates, on cultivating a sexual sanctity defined by the limits set by these *mitzvot*, and using certain times of the year (and, ideally, a central place) as specific vehicles of sustaining and furthering the relationship with God.

That picture comes out of the prohibitive approach to the religion, and yet fully coheres with what we saw earlier. In the next chapter, we will look at the most prominent of the religion's obligations, and see if that takes us to the same place.

Chapter 9

Ubiquitous *Mitzvot*

What we are required to avoid does not yet necessarily teach us what the religion seeks most as a positive value. Prohibitions outline the negative space of religion, the relationship with God formed by that from which we *refrain*; the obligations set up a more active relationship in requiring Jews to *do* something.

Here, too, we need a way to measure significance, to see whether some *mitzvot* stand out as more central, more vital to the religion's concerns, than others. We cannot rely on punishments as a marker of importance, since only two positive commandments are punished in the severe manner we highlighted in the previous chapter. Those two — the willful failure to offer the Paschal sacrifice or to be circumcised (for men) — are indeed important, but leave out others that should also be in that list.

Level of repentance required for transgression, which helped us last chapter, also fails here. As we saw, atoning for the failure to fulfill positive commandments is in fact easier than even "ordinary" prohibitions, since it comes through repentance alone. Worse than leaving us without a way to judge importance, it might suggest obligations are actually religiously less important than prohibitions.

Could the Positive Be More Shaping of Religiosity Than the Prohibited?

One *halachic* principle points us in the other direction. Although the specifics are complicated and not our issue, there is a rule that עשה דוחה לא תעשה, that if a simple prohibition stands in the way of fulfilling an obligation, the commandment "pushes aside" the prohibition. One example comes from the laws of *tsitsit*, the strings placed at the corners of any garment that has four or more corners.

Some of those strings (the exact number is a matter of debate) are supposed to be dyed with תכלת, a bluish color. *Techelet*-dyed strings are made of wool, but garments of either wool or linen are obligated in *tsitsit*. Putting woolen strings on a linen garment seems to violate the prohibition of שעטנז, *shatnez*, of weaving wool and linen together. The principle of עשה דוחה לא תעשה explains how this is allowed: the commandment of *tsitsit* pushes aside the prohibition against wearing *shatnez*.[1]

That positive commandments can sometimes override prohibitions shows us that severity of punishment is not the only way to judge religious significance. I suspect this is because obligations fill in the content of a religious personality. The prohibitions tell us only what is off-limits, what damages religiosity, but do not actively advance our connection to God, except insofar as avoiding what is wrong removes flaws that make us more God-like. Positive commandments open doors to a deeper and richer interaction with the Creator.

That would explain why repentance alone suffices — the failure to fulfill an obligation is a missed opportunity, whereas transgressions are actual wrongs that must be rectified. If I fail to invest, I have missed the chance to make money, but if I steal, I am in possession of money that does not rightfully belong to me. Sins need to be atoned; lost chances need only to be regretted and taken off the table as candidates for future neglect.

---

1. *Betsah* 8b. אנצקלופדיה תלמודית, the Talmudic Encyclopedia, vol. 2, p. 81, notes that we generally assume that a positive commandment cannot push aside a *karet* prohibition, again highlighting the severity of this class of prohibitions, as in the previous chapter.

Back to Ubiquity as a Marker

Just as we saw the greater centrality of those texts and ideas that the Torah insisted should stay in our consciousnesses continuously or at least continually, we can identify *mitzvot* that are more consistently part of a Jewish life than others, more deeply molding the character of Judaism.

Two such lists point us in that exact direction. First, *Sefer HaChinuch*, the thirteenth-century discussion of the Torah's commandments, notes that six of the 613 commandments apply to all Jews, male or female, at all times of their lives, without break or pause, regardless of geographical location or historical era. Clearly, such timeless and universal obligations are foundational to a Jew's relationship with God.

However we define Judaism and how a Jew should see his or her role in the world, these six have to be prominent, since they are what the system demands of all Jews all the time. The six are:

(1) to believe in God,
(2) to refrain from believing any force or power in the universe can compete with God,
(3) to believe in God's Unity,
(4) to love God,
(5) to fear God, and
(6) not to stray after the thoughts of one's hearts or after one's eyes.

The first three commandments make points about belief we discussed earlier, so I will not belabor them here. I will only note that much of Jewish *belief* turns out to be *legislated*, meaning that being always aware of those beliefs is a plain legal imperative. It is a matter of Jewish *law*, not faith, to continuingly and continuously believe in God, to refrain from believing in any competing powers, and to assert God's unity.

More, these laws obligate every moment of every Jewish life. This should, it seems to me, be a final death-knell for almost any version of Orthopraxy; even if a person chooses to claim that

Orthodoxy is about *halachic* practice, such practice requires — at all moments of every Jewish life throughout history — holding these beliefs actively.

I also note that these commandments necessitate some discussion of the nature of God and other such issues. To claim to believe in, love, or fear God does not qualify as fulfillment of these commandments unless the God being believed in, loved, or feared, is the One Jewish tradition asserts, with all the characteristics we saw in the Principles of Faith. To believe in a triune God, for example, is not just a violation of the Principle that God is unitary, it means that all of that person's efforts to love and fear God are focused on a God that doesn't exist.

Active Involvement With, Not Just Belief In, God

The other three commandments show us that, as a matter of Jewish law, faith requires more than an internal experience. Love and fear are emotions that must shape how we act, so that a Jew is always required to be relating to God, at each second of his or her day. The multiple ways to accomplish this cannot be boiled down to specific acts or paragraphs of a code — nor can it be fully delineated by other *halachot* — which is perhaps why people do not recognize them as *halachah*. And even so, they are.

Perhaps the best expression of this is Rambam's description of how such a life might look, in *Deot* (Laws of Character Traits) 3:3. He notes that even ordinary bodily activities can be part of fostering one's relationship with God as long as they are undertaken for that purpose. I can sleep, go on vacation, or eat a fine steak for the pure enjoyment, or I can do those (and other) activities out of a considered and sincere judgment of how they will enhance and advance my service of God.

There is a Hasidic story that makes this point, although I confess I have forgotten the names of the heroes. Whoever they were, a *rebbe*, an Hasidic master, and his student were each about to eat an apple. As they sat looking at their apples, the student (who comes across as not so much of a *hasid*, so it's perhaps better I've forgotten his name) thought to himself, "Really, how is the *rebbe* so different from me? He eats and I eat."

The *rebbe*, being a *rebbe*, intuited the other's thoughts, and asked that very question. When the *hasid* admitted he did not see the difference, the *rebbe* said, "I'll tell you. You decide you would enjoy an apple, and to allow yourself that pleasure, make a blessing beforehand. I decide I would enjoy blessing my Father in Heaven, and to get to that pleasure, I eat an apple."

The commandments of love and fear tell a Jew the questions that should frame all of his or her activities — is thinking this thought, performing this act, or indulging this pleasure promoting a better relationship with God, neutral, or, Heaven forefend, a contradiction of what God wants of me? Whatever the answer, the questioning itself is part of keeping the fulfillment of these commandments in mind throughout our lives.

Safeguards and Their Role

The final *mitzvah* in the six, as ubiquitous as the others, warns Jews to continuously and continuingly avoid enticements that take us away from God, intellectual or appetitive. With the mind the seat of thinking and the eyes the vehicles of desire, the last of the constant *mitzvot* adjures the Jew to recognize the frequent, perhaps constant, distractions the world presents. It is not enough to resist spiritual dangers as they come along; לא תתורו tells us to be ever alert, to avoid any path that even might lead to such temptations.

Note that the individuality of what tempts us makes specifics impossible. What is unequivocal is Jews' need to always recognize the *possibility* that an idea or bodily pleasure will engender thoughts or feelings that run counter to a God-centered world. That recognition translates into a need to critically evaluate all ideas and pleasures we imbibe, to see not only whether some specific *halachah* rules them out, but also whether they lure a person, either intellectually or appetitively, away from God.

A story about the late R. Shlomo Carlebach makes the point

well, I believe. In the 1960s, he founded his House of Peace and Love in San Francisco in an attempt, as far as I know, to give disaffected Jews a path back to God. One of his students recalls that he ingested a lot of drugs during his time there.

He relates that R. Carlebach saw him one morning and said something along the lines of, "If it brought you closer to Hashem, I wouldn't say anything; but as it is, you stay up late, miss the Torah study classes, and are unable to think straight." Whether or not drugs violate a specific paragraph in the codes, he was saying, they demonstrably take a person away (in that case, both intellectually *and* appetitively) from service of God.

These six *mitzvot* already shape a worldview considerably more God-focused than even many Orthodox Jews currently realize. The six envision Jewish life as one of constant devotion to the One God, both in the sense that there are no others and the sense of unity intended by the Shema. That devotion should express itself, at least, in a desire to grow in both positive (loving) and awe-filled (fearing) aspects of the relationship and of an awareness of the possible threats to that devotion the world tends to present, to be ever alert to those dangers, and to resist them when they come close.

As I have noted before, these obligations also mean that whatever else the religion wants of us *expands* on these six, not competes with them. Any expression of Judaism that fails to place the six front and center is, by that very fact, essentially lacking.

I think we could stop here and much of my point would have been made, that the commandments of the Torah bring us to a very similar place to where we found ourselves before. By looking at one more list of commandments, those that Rambam notes obligate all male Jews at some point in their lives (there is a shorter, but similar, list for women, as we will see), we can expand and deepen our recognition of what the religion is supposed to be about.

Chapter 10

Sixty Obligations That Characterize Ordinary Jewish Life

Rambam tells us that prior to writing his code of Jewish law, the *Mishneh Torah*, he wrote his *Sefer haMitzvot* — Book of the Commandments, which enumerates the 613 commandments of the Torah — to ensure that he not omit anything in his presentation. He separates the commandments into obligations and prohibitions and closes his presentation of the 248 obligations by noting that sixty apply to all male Jews in all places at some point in the course of an ordinary life. Forty-six of those are incumbent on women as well.

Both lists, the sixty for men and forty-six for women, further fortify the claim that Judaism — and all the *halachot* that clarify how to fulfill its dictates — is more about God and the relationship with God than anything else, and that the essential concerns of the religion have always focused on that. I should note that, as with Behag's list of death and *karet* penalty prohibitions, elements of Maimonides' list are disputed — he counts *mitzvot* others would not and vice versa — but not enough to weaken the conclusions.

As before, a *mitzvah*-by-*mitzvah* discussion would take too long and necessarily rest on personal interpretations. I mention this again to remind readers that limiting ourselves to that which is unequivocally true, with all its advantages, cannot be confused with a delineation of a full experience of a personal or communal Orthodoxy. What we are finding here is not the whole of the picture; it is the necessary and indispensable central part of that picture. The surprise, I hope I am showing, is how far we have gotten from even that.

Rambam presents the sixty in the order in which they appeared in his enumeration of the *mitzvot,* which follows an internal logic that would not be apparent in reading only these sixty. I instead regroup them by the themes I believe they highlight. While I acknowledge that this prejudices the presentation, I hope readers will agree the patterns I see jump out of the list on their own, rather than my imposing them on that list.

Building Awareness of God

The first nine *mitzvot* in Rambam's list are: to believe in God (a First Cause),[1] to believe in the unity of, to love, and to fear God, to serve/worship God (through prayer, Torah study, and in other ways), to cling to Torah scholars as an expression of clinging/cleaving to God, to swear in God's Name, to imitate God (or God's Attributes) to the extent possible, and to sanctify God's Name, which includes working to spread belief in God throughout the world.

It would be easy to skim the list and fail to notice its significance. Of the sixty obligations that apply to all male Jewish lives at some point, fifteen percent for men (and almost twenty percent for women) define a framework to build awareness of and connection to God. These *mitzvot* tell us both that we need to build a life in relationship with God and much of the *how* of doing that.

While some of these are hard to define with the *halachic* exactness so many of us crave — some might see Torah study as the highest road to love, others might find love of God in understanding the workings of the universe or performing acts of kindness — the obligation to build a relationship with Torah scholars is

---

1. Behag omits this *mitzvah.* Ramban, the 13th century Talmudist who glossed Rambam's Book of Mitzvot, and others note that the belief in God is actually the necessary foundation for all the other commandments and therefore could not be a commandment of its own. That they agree on the basic necessity of such a belief suffices for our purposes here.

more clear and yet, in my experience, fails to make the agenda of many observant Jews. So, too, tradition assumed imitating God's Attributes primarily took the form of acts of justice and kindness, old friends from earlier chapters.

Finally, at least for Rambam, part of sanctifying God's Name is attempting to spread the knowledge and awareness of God. Granted, others — such as the Tosafists — understood that obligation only as an issue of refusing to abandon observance in the face of persecution. Either version, though, does insist on the commitment to serving as a witness to God's truth, always or when absolutely necessary.

Practical Tools for Awareness

Seven more *mitzvot*, bringing us to over a quarter of the list, institute specific practices explicity geared towards leading us to awareness of God. They are: to recite Shema morning and evening, to wear head and hand *tefillin* and *tsitsit* (women are not obligated in any of these), to place *mezuzot* on doorposts, to bless God after eating (which may include women),[2] and that the male priests should bless the people every day.

While much of priests' role in Jewish society was lost with the destruction of the Temple, this last obligation as well as two more in the list — the requirement to honor male priests and to give a male or female priest certain parts of slaughtered animals — suggests priests serve a dual role, reminding us of the continuing lack of a Temple as well as serving as living representatives of God.

Two other commandments, to study Torah and to teach it, and that each man own (preferably write) a Torah scroll of his own, also seem focused on awareness of God, but leave enough room for debate that I will not insist on the point. However we conceive of those, just about a third of Rambam's list either directly

---

2. Rambam does not exclude women, although the Talmud is uncertain as to whether women's obligation in Grace After Meals stems from Torah law or rabbinic ordinance.

mandates building a connection with God or sets up required frameworks for such connection to occur.

This is worth remarking and repeating: About a *third* of the obligations that are part of every Jewish life revolve around awareness of God and actions taken to foster it. That should, it seems to me, translate into Jews being people who stand out in society for their focus on God. One of the first things people should say about Jews — not rabbis or other clergy, but simple Jews — it would seem to mean, is "Oh, they're so focused on God."

The Holidays

Seventeen more *mitzvot* — almost thirty percent of the list — focus on holy days, Shabbat and the holidays. These *mitzvot* are: to rejoice on the Festivals; to desist from creative work on the Sabbath; to sanctify the Sabbath with words; to remove leavened bread from our houses on the fourteenth of Nisan; to tell the story of the Exodus on the night of the fifteenth of Nisan; to eat *matsah* that night; to desist from prohibited labor on the first and seventh day of Passover; to count forty-nine days from the cutting of the Omer; to desist from prohibited labor on Shavuot, on the first day of Tishrei, on the tenth day of Tishrei, when we also have to afflict our souls; to desist from labor on the first and eighth day of Sukkot; to reside in a Sukkah for seven days; to take a *lulav* and celebrate with it before God for seven days (although only one day outside the Temple); and to hear the *shofar* on Rosh haShanah. Of those, Omer, *Sukkah*, *lulav*, and *shofar* are not incumbent on women.

What seems unequivocal is that a Jew's year includes periodic days of withdrawing from the world to focus on some aspect of the relationship with God (the memory of the Exodus, the experience of the desert, the offering of new grains in the Temple on Shavuot, etc.). These days are defined by both general obligations to desist from creative labor as well as specific ritual acts that give shape and substance to the messages of the day.

Once the holidays are included, we find that well over half

of Rambam's list of *mitzvot* that accompany an ordinary Jewish life, male or female, serve to shape and focus that Jew's attention on God. Granting the room for differences of interpretation and nuance, we once again find ourselves, in a fully *halachic* context, seeing just how central the focus on God is in a well-conceived Jewish life.

Family and Society

A further fourteen commandments — almost a quarter of the list — regulate the functioning of civil society at large, and family life in particular. These commandments are: to follow the majority in disputes among the sages; to remove dangers from society (the Torah's specific example was constructing a fence around our roofs, but Rambam understood it to incorporate the broader imperative); to do charity and sustain the weak; to lend money to a poor person; to love our fellow Jews; to love converts; to correct weights and measures as much as possible; to honor Sages, at least by standing for them; to honor our parents; to fear our parents; to procreate (at least one boy and one girl, a commandment not obligatory upon women); to perform *kiddushin* (giving the bride a ring or other object of value to cement her sole connection to her husband) before marrying; to have the groom stay with his bride — meaning, not to travel outside the city without her permission or to go to war — for the first year of marriage; and the father's obligation to circumcise his sons.

The society these commandments envision seems focused on fostering respect for authority — social, religious, and parental — and the rule of the majority balanced with bonds of love and concern extending both to ordinary and disadvantaged members of that society, and the creation and sustenance of families.

Families are consciously created by marriage ceremonies, as opposed to just living together — which Rambam accepted as a valid way to create binding marriages among non-Jews — are concerned with building a bond between husband and wife at the relationship's onset, and are at least partially focused on the bearing of children and raising them with a sense of their attachment to the Jewish people (the *mitzvah* of circumcision). Those children, in turn, owe their parents a constant awareness of their role in their creation.

Taken together, 85 percent of Rambam's list consists of commandments that develop a relationship with God, use holidays to intensify some aspect of that relationship, and build a society that can promote its members' abilities to flourish in their God-centered lives. It is no wonder he tells us in Guide III:27 that all the *mitzvot* in the Torah contribute either to תקון הנפש, the welfare of the soul, or תקון הגוף, the welfare of the body — the simplest readings of the most prominent *mitzvot* point that way!

Closing Up and Summarizing the List

Other interesting aspects of Rambam's list are beyond my scope here, such as why he counts separate obligations to check the kosher signs of any animals, birds, or fish that we eat[3] — that it

---

3. Or why he skipped *mitzvah* 151, the obligation to check the signs of grasshoppers and similar insects, which appears in between obligations he did include, to check the signs of birds and fish. Possibly, Rambam expected people to eat meat, birds, and fish during an ordinary life but not grasshoppers, although we know of no reason that should be so.

I personally believe this oddity should be paired with another one, that Rambam included *mitzvah* 172 in his list, the obligation to listen to prophets. Since Judaism last saw recognized prophets at the beginning of the Second Temple, *mitzvah* 172 sticks out in a list of those that apply in all times to an ordinary Jewish life. Rambam may have assumed there were prophets in every generation, which would be revolutionary and interesting in its own way. Famously, the late Abraham Joshua Heschel suggested that Rambam may have thought of himself as a prophet; if that were true, it would fit well here.

My own suspicion, with no evidence to back it up, is that Rambam wrote 151, קנ"א in Hebrew letters, and an early copyist misread it as קע"ב 172. That would mean, though, that aside from misreading the letters, the copyist moved *mitzvah* 151 to the place for 172. Still, it explains both otherwise odd aspects of the list.

was prohibited to eat those foods would seem to require such checking, without the need for a positive commandment. Since others, such as Behag, do not recognize these as separate obligations, however, we leave that for another time.

It *is* unequivocally true, though, that just about all the limitations on *which* foods we can eat focus on the animal world. Other than issues of tithing and insect infestations, grains, fruits, and vegetables are unregulated by Torah food law. This suggests that the food aspect of *mitzvot* was concerned with regulating how Jews partook of the animal world, not food in general, another topic worthy of consideration.

The three *mitzvot* on Rambam's list we have yet to mention, to articulate/confess our sins along with our repentance, to fulfill our oaths, and to listen to/obey a prophet, are open to differing interpretations,[4] so I leave them for another time as well.

Without pretending to have mined the wealth of ideas and insights each of these commandments could provide, I think we can accurately if incompletely say that this subset of *mitzvot*, akin to the other sources we have consulted, presents Judaism as a religion focused on shaping people to know God, to be aware of God (daily and in periodic intensive holidays), and to apply that awareness to every facet of their lives, such as the communities and families they establish and the food they eat.

Building my confidence in these conclusions is that we have found them in each place we looked. Whether we built a view of Judaism from within Scripture — as in the texts to remember daily, the theology implied by the *haftarot*, or the Talmud's understanding of the Prophets' encapsulations of *mitzvot* — from Principles of Faith as articulated by Rambam and then discussed for centuries, or from different slices of the world of Jewish law, we always meet the same basic ideas and principles.

---

4. Rambam had assumed there was a *mitzvah* to swear in the Name of God, so accepting the absolute need to fulfill the oath would be a function of our desire to avoid denigrating God's Name by neglecting commitments to which we attached that Name.

Women and Their Exemptions[5]

That characterization of what we found, I find it important to note, is true of women as well, even though they are not obligated in fourteen of the sixty. Interestingly, Rambam seems to have been alert to this difference, as he offers two mnemonics to remember the number of women's *mitzvot* as opposed to men's. First, he cites the verse כי אזלת יד, that the hand has fallen away,[6] the numerological value of the word יד, hand, being fourteen, and then he notes גם את בדם בריתך, you, too, in the blood of your covenant,[7] where the word בדם, in the blood, numbers forty-six.

The mnemonics have contrasting implications. The first sees women's obligations as lesser than men's, a יד or fourteen, having fallen away. In the second, Rambam seems to indicate that women have a forty-six-*mitzvah* covenant of their own (בדם בריתך, in the blood of *your* covenant) that would be equivalent to men's despite its differences.

That separate women's covenant, judging from the list, focuses on larger religious ideals, not on their specific manifestations. Women are not required to lay head and hand *tefillin* or wear *tsitsit*, but bear equal responsibility to believe in, think about, imitate, and serve God. So, too, they are exempt from specific manifestations of holidays — *shofar, sukkah, lulav*, counting the Omer — but are fully obligated in the days themselves.[8]

I will return to this in the second part, but what we have seen already suggests that one axis along which women and men

---

5. There are other factors that differentiate the religion's treatment of the two sexes, such as the different ways the requirements of צניעות, modesty, affect each. I do not mean here to completely explain women's role in Judaism, just to note one aspect of the question for which Rambam's list suggests an answer.
6. *Devarim* 32:36.
7. *Zechariah* 9:11.
8. Their exemption from the commandments relating to family — the groom staying with his bride for a year, the obligation to have children, and to circumcise boys — suggests that they were not held responsible for family-creation, a topic for a different discussion.

differ is the specificity with which the religion chooses to shape their relationship with God. A woman may observe the holidays exactly as men do, in which case she will experience her status as אזלת יד, lacking obligations men have. But Rambam implies that a woman might equally forge her own holiday path, which might not include sitting in a *sukkah* or shaking a *lulav*, and develop her own sense of how to celebrate what God did for the Jewish people in the desert. For such a woman, her covenant would be בדם בריתך, a forty-six-part connection to God.

So here is our concise restatement of the core of Jewish belief and practice: Jews are meant to live in constant awareness of the God Who took the Jews out of Egypt; of the event at Sinai in which God communicated directly with a man and commanded the Torah and all of its laws; and of God's promise to reward and punish successes and failures, respectively, of that observance and awareness. Central foci of those observances are looking to serve God at every turn, denying or rejecting all temptations to act in ways other than for the service of God (including, notably, wrongful sexuality), and building families, communities, and a nation that shares those ideals.

The clearest next step would be to show how that view differs practically from how Jews today live their lives, and I will get there, but I have several further steps to take. The first, in the next chapter, is to discuss religiously vital aspects of Judaism that were not on our list.

Chapter 11

Important, But Not Central
or Unequivocal

Despite my general interest in discussing only that which is unequivocal, I need to briefly take up three other aspects of Jewish life, the roles of *halachic* process — meaning, the way we decide what constitutes authoritative Jewish law — the Land of Israel, and *minhag*, or custom. The first is central to a Jewish life but not unequivocal, the second is unequivocal but not as central as I mean the term here, and the third is neither. Let me elaborate for each.

Defining What God Wants of Us: The Vital Role of *Halachic* Process

One possible objection to my summary so far is that it might equally describe certain conscientious and God-focused Christians, Muslims, and even Jews of different denominations. Justice, kindness, and mercy can sound too apple-pie, not Jewishly individualized enough.

I do not want to gloss over or minimize the value I find in so many people striving to perform acts of justice, kindness, and mercy, many of them explicitly linking it to their desire to serve God. But I emphasize that, important as their actions are and as much good as they bring, traditional Judaism articulates a different perspective of these ideals, so that what might seem like justice and mercy to some can, from a proper Jewish perspective, be actually wrong. Until we as Jews help inaugurate a world that defines those terms accurately, we will not have succeeded at the task God set for us.

That Jewish view, often similar to but equally often distinct from and even at odds with the non-Jewish one,[1] is defined by *halachah*. I have mentioned *halachah* many times before, but here the important part of that stress is that *halachah* is the only place to find accurate definitions and/or parameters of Jewish obligations and ideals.

To take a few simple examples, the laws of idol worship make certain unequivocal statements about Whom we are allowed to worship and how. Someone who strives to build a relationship with God in prohibited ways, no matter how sincerely or assiduously, misses the mark. The definition of charity and justice also hinges on *halachic* decisions: what might seem a charitable act, such as letting a poor man fail to pay back a loan, is, if *halachah* prohibits it, actually a perversion of the system, a deep sin rather than a great merit.

The same is true for more technical *mitzvot*, such as eating *matsah* or telling the Exodus story on the night of Passover. Performing those acts in a way *halachah* does not recognize constitutes a failure to fulfill that obligation, once again despite sincerity or assiduousness. Harsh as that sounds — and I grant that I, too, hope and expect God is not so strict as to completely ignore a person's attempts, no matter how misconceived — if one eats a rice cake as *matsah*, the desire to fulfill God's command might be great, but that person will not have eaten *matsah* that Passover eve.

In defining our obligations — including, especially, the ones that sit at the core of the Jewish view of the world — *halachah* is clearly central and indispensable to a properly lived life. And yet I have said almost nothing here about how we go about discovering what God requires of us.

---

1. I demonstrated some of those differences, for the most apparently intuitive commandments, in my "Involuntary Particularism: The Noahide Laws, Citizenship, and Alienage," 18 *Geo. Immigr. L.J.* 543.

Central, But Not Unequivocal

The reason for that, one I bemoan, is that I know of no way to define *halachah* unequivocally. I have shared some of my own thoughts on what constitutes authoritative *halachah* or even proper *halachic* thinking elsewhere, but I again refrain from including personal impressions.[2] While the *Shulchan Aruch* is often authoritative, it is not always so, nor is it comprehensive. While certain great decisors have become broadly accepted on most questions — such as the late R. Moshe Feinstein, ob"m — they are neither universally accepted in all segments of Judaism nor on all topics they addressed.

We are left with a deep quandary, one that seems to me to endanger a unified sense of the religion. While most of Orthodoxy has rejected other denominations' sense of Jewish law, there is growing disagreement *within* Orthodoxy as to what constitutes valid law and legal process. Some who identify as Orthodox decide *halachic* issues in ways I find illegitimate, much as others would probably say the same about me.

This is an intensely distressing situation that needs addressing, but not here. Here, as I seek to lay out only what is unequivocal, I cannot say anything more specific about how to rule on *halachic* questions. We can long for a return to the times of the Sanhedrin, when the parameters of acceptability could be hashed out and decided in a manner that binds the entire Jewish people, but until then we are left with the recognition that the proper definition of the terms we have been using resides in a *halachah* that cannot be unequivocally defined at the current time.

Living in Israel: A Value Independent of Zionism

Readers of an earlier draft of this book noted that I have failed to mention the obligation to live in Israel, an odd omission for someone with strong positive feelings towards both the Land and the State

---

2. See my Mission of Orthodoxy posts, blog.webyeshiva.org, posts 19–21.

of Israel. For what we might call a card-carrying Zionist, wouldn't living in Israel seem to be part of the mission of the religion?

To explain why my answer is "no," let me start by noting that Zionism has obscured an important unequivocal truth of the religion. What we call Zionism, the movement beginning in the late nineteenth century to encourage Jewish settlement of the Land of Israel, was spearheaded mostly by nonobservant Jews who came to their attachment to a Jewish homeland in ways that were not obviously or directly related to Torah and its values. Even as some leaders of observant Jewry came to embrace the phenomenon despite its downsides, forming what we call Religious Zionism, many and probably most others felt that observant Jews should not join in this movement.

We can feel what we want about that — and we should doubt our 20/20 hindsight if we feel too certain of our criticism of our forebears — but those historical events are irrelevant to the undeniable Jewish importance of living in Israel. None of those rabbis disagreed about the great value Judaism places on living in Israel; the debate at the time — continuing today, in a different way — was on when and how to push to move back to Israel as well as the propriety of cooperating with the nonreligious.

It is for that reason, for example, that the contemporary State of Israel sees more and more right-wing Jews living there; now that the framework has been established, the importance of residence in the Land for a fully-lived Jewish life is obvious to all.

Importance Might not Indicate Centrality

It should not be necessary, but let me briefly review some sources that declare the value of living in Israel. Most prominently, it seems to me, is that the Torah revolves to a large degree around getting Avraham's descendants back there. God had promised the Land to the first Patriarch, and the Exodus's ultimate goal was fulfilling that promise. So, too, Moshe Rabbenu prays vigorously to be allowed to enter the Land.

There is also firm *halachic* evidence. In an example we all should hope stays theoretical, *halachah* is clear that either spouse in a marriage can insist on moving to Israel with financial benefits.[3] Ramban states the matter more simply, adding a *mitzvah* to live in Israel to his list of those Rambam neglected to include. As is well-known, Ramban made his way to Israel towards the end of his life, a fulfillment of the *mitzvah* as he saw it.

Rambam's not counting it as a *mitzvah* is one reason we could not argue that living in Israel was central, or at least not unequivocally so, but Rambam does cite many of the Talmudic sources that stress the importance of living in Israel. He records the Talmud's statement that one may only leave Israel to study Torah, marry, or to salvage property and then return.

He goes on in that vein, noting the Sages' practice of rolling in the dirt of the Land and kissing its borders, the value even of being buried in Israel, and so on.[4] This leaves the question of why he did not include it as a *mitzvah*, but none of the numerous answers suggested has been universally accepted, so we will not enter that discussion here.

So, Part of the Point, Right?

I admit I have no problem with someone saying they see living in the Land as essential to their Jewishness. What stops me from including it is that we and our ancestors have lived outside of Israel for thousands of years as punishment for our sins. Many if not most of those Jews built lives of faith and commitment to God, many of them giants of Torah and/or righteous in a way I could hardly aspire towards, let alone accomplish. I cannot imagine implying they were excluded from the minimal expression of the religion.

---

3. *Ketubbot* 110b and *Shulchan Aruch Even haEzer* 75:3–4 note that if the marriage breaks up over this, the financial prejudice rules against the spouse opposed to going, as long as there is no suspicion that the move to Israel is fraudulent, a means of securing the divorce on better terms than otherwise.
4. See his *Hilchot Melachim* 5:9–12.

A story captures this dichotomy. R. Ben-Zion Gold, ob"m, a mid-twentieth-century Orthodox Zionist, was touring the United States to raise money. When in Baltimore, he stayed at the home of R. Yitshak Ruderman, ob"m, a friend from European *yeshivot* who had gone on to found a non-Zionist *yeshiva*, Ner Israel.

A listener asked R. Gold why he stayed at the home of a non-Zionist, glossing over the uncomfortable truth that the Zionists of Baltimore (at the time) were insufficiently observant to properly host a man of R. Gold's *halachic* commitments. R. Gold responded, "Because with him I have a dispute over one *mitzvah* (the settling of the Land of Israel). With you, I have a dispute over many more."

This is not to downplay — and I believe non-Zionists would have to agree — that Jewish experience is always significantly lacking outside of Israel, especially in the absence of a Temple and the related laws that come into play in those circumstances. This is the condition of Jewish Diaspora, partially alleviated by events of the last century and a half, but that still awaits the full Redemption, speedily in our days.[5]

Minhag: The Behemoth That Overtakes Us

Jews, like all humans, do not live by theory alone. "Real" world Judaism is rarely if ever expressed as the sources call for it. As R. Joseph B. Soloveitchik, ob"m, once noted, when learned husbands suggest to their wives that they need not be stringent in certain areas of the dietary laws, the wives kick them out of the kitchen, insistent on tradition as passed along. This focus on custom and tradition, positive in many ways, carries the danger of warping the system, giving certain practices and expressions of religiosity a centrality the system never intended.

In saying that, I do not want to seem to be dismissive of custom. Indeed, Talmudic tradition thought Scripture required

---

5. Of course, the Redemption itself might occur in stages, as I imagined in my *Murderer in the Mikdash*.

us to follow custom, citing either a verse from Haazinu — which, as we saw earlier, is a central text of the religion — or one from Proverbs. Nonetheless, custom often attains a centrality it clearly does not deserve, and besides, the proper role of custom is not unequivocally laid out in traditional sources.

Jews often define their observance by customary markers rather than *halachic* ones. On the more "left" side of religiosity, we find Jews who consider themselves and others observant as long as they keep the dietary laws or attend a particular kind of synagogue, even though neither of those — important as they are — could be seen as central to religiosity or observance.

On the "right," this same process sometimes leads to defining Orthodoxy as wearing curly sidelocks (for men) or a certain style of hair covering and/or skirt for women. In an extreme (and distressing) example, a friend told me of a young man who grew up in a "right-wing" Israeli family, for the purposes of this story defined by its opposition to serving in the Israeli Army.

The young man decided to attend a *yeshivat hesder*, a post-high school institution in which he would combine Torah study time and army service; other than ceding some Torah time to army service, the commitment to observance and Torah study is, at least in theory, the same as in the "right-wing" world. The father cut him off since, to him, the son had abandoned the religion and values he had been taught at home and refused to speak with him.

One of the boy's aunts took him in so that he could have a place to go on occasions when he got time off from the Army base and/or *yeshiva*; the father stopped speaking with her as well. For that father, army service was a mark of having left Orthodoxy.

We could add to these examples, but they all share the flaw of defining religiosity sociologically, not out of a well-founded consideration of what *halachah* itself says.

Drifting with Sociology

To come to more common examples of sociology outweighing religion, we need only look at synagogues. Consider the day before

Passover, where custom decreed first-born males should fast to commemorate their having escaped the fate of the Egyptian first-born. Observing that in the breech, first-borns today gather in large numbers to hear a *siyyum*, a completion of some significant piece of Torah study, allowing them to partake of a meal and thus exempt themselves from fasting.

Similarly, the first night of *selichot*, of reciting customary pleas for forgiveness in the days leading up to Rosh haShanah and Yom Kippur, draws numbers not only much greater than synagogue services that are more *halachically* significant, but also than the rest of the *selichot* up until Yom Kippur. It is not the urge to make peace with God that is uppermost for many of these people, but the custom to attend these services.

Speaking of Yom Kippur, *Kol Nidre*, the beginning of the services on Yom Kippur eve, draws many more people than other prayers of that very day. As with the other examples, *Kol Nidre* has little, if any, *halachic* meaning, and is thus completely a matter of sociology, of how people are used to experiencing their Day of Atonement.

One final example is *Yizkor* and *kaddish*, prayers recited in memory of deceased relatives. Here, too, people who otherwise make no particular attempt to attend synagogue go out of their way to be there all the time and on time.

It is not that this or any of the other customs lack attestation in Jewish tradition; it is that the level of commitment they inspire, in contrast to practices with greater systemic value, reminds us that for many Jews, including Orthodox ones, the *system*'s wants are not paramount in determining how to act.

The most uncomfortable element of this reality, to me, is that it seems to ratify the views of Mordechai Kaplan, who was expelled from Orthodox rabbinic circles for arguing that Judaism is a culture rather than a religion and developed Reconstructionist Judaism based on that insight. Common practice today suggests Kaplan accurately reported the way too many Jews experience their religion; his error was going from description to prescription, from *is* to *ought*.

Not Only Not Central

There are positive values to following custom as well,[6] but those are not my concern here. As a first step, it was important for us to remember that whatever custom properly is (as was true for *halachic* process and living in Israel as well), it cannot compete with, or replace, an awareness of the core interests of the religion.

Custom's overwhelming claim on Jews' devotion also does not pass the basic test by which I have tried to evaluate candidates for our discussion, unequivocality. Custom, by its very nature, defines the practice of subsets of Jews either by location or familial tradition. There is also significant debate about what constitutes a custom, when a custom can change, and what determines the custom that an individual must, should, or can follow.[7] Whatever the answers to those questions, they lay out a map of how Jews can differ and individualize their religiosity. This has value as well, as we will discuss in the next part of this book, but here it demonstrates that custom can only be ancillary to the trunk of Jewish religiosity, the core that ought to define all Jews.

Custom does, however, productively lead us into the next section of this discussion, where I try to show the extent to which God sought to leave us room to make personal decisions about how to best express the central ideas of our task on earth. While I could pause here and show how the unequivocal parts of the religion would change its modern expression, I will be able to do that more thoroughly after engaging that next discussion, to which I now turn.

---

6. See my Mission of Orthodoxy, post 22 available at http://blog.webye-shiva.org/orthodoxy/the-mission-of-orthodoxy-project-no-22-the-way-people-live-and-its-impact-on-the-mission.

7. I have taken up some of these issues ibid., post 23 available at http://blog.webyeshiva.org/orthodoxy/the-mission-of-orthodoxy-project-no-23-finishing-up-with-minhag-and-then-putting-the-mission-into-practice.

Part II

The Necessity
of Autonomy

Chapter 12

Finding Our Own Paths
in Serving God

Introduction: The Question of *Mitzvot*

In the first part of this work, I articulated a definition of the core of Judaism shared by a wide range of sources. Part of my point was that *halachah*, Jewish law, sets out so many ideals to strive towards that we can lose sight of the overall thrust of the religion. In very short sum, I tried to emphasize that our observance of *halachah* must always contribute to service of God, the true goal of human life, characterized chiefly by our attempting to shape our personal selves and our societies in more God-like and God-focused ways.

I was at pains to stress that I did not mean that awareness of this core could replace striving for the ideal, just that it needed to always figure in how we shaped our religious efforts so that we not lose sight of our overall goals. As can happen in life in general, we could get so caught up in the building blocks of a religious life that we forget what those blocks were aimed at constructing.

While that offers one kind of corrective to what can sometimes turn into a misguided focus on ritual as the sole arbiter of a proper Jewish life, I wish here to offer another. In that part, I was pointing out that *halachah*, internally, has goals and ideals that should always shape our observance of the Torah; it is insufficient, I was showing, to justify the lives we lead by saying we are following *halachah*. Rather, we must be able always to say we are following *halachah* in the overall directions it was trying to lead us.

Here, I go one step further, showing that while *halachah* is indispensable to proper service of God, it is also necessarily insufficient to that project. That is, even a Jew who observed *all* of *halachah* would be forced by the system itself to make personal choices about how to live his or her Jewish life, choices not fully defined or constrained by *halachic* input. Traditional sources, I maintain, show that God insists *we* choose how best to express our connection to the Divine.

Certainly *halachah* and *hashkafa* (Jewish thought) offer indispensable guidance as to how to do that, but significant aspects of a well-lived life are almost entirely personal, for each of us to figure out for ourselves. I mean to show, then, that *halachah* is more of a framework than the be-all, end-all for which it is sometimes taken.

Isn't It Obvious?

While I am most interested in this idea because it is true and it shows us untapped fields of religious excellence where we could roam free, it also contributes to solving a problem many have with Judaism. Particularly in democracies, people today are acutely aware of their own importance, value their personal opinions, and value their right to choose their paths in life. Many, then, resist the notion that religion tells us exactly what to do, and perhaps therefore try to limit religion's sphere of influence.

In philosophy, Immanuel Kant highlighted the problem when he derided Judaism's inferiority on these very grounds. In his view, Judaism wants obedience, whereas Kant insisted that other-commanded acts cannot be as morally valuable as personally chosen and free-willed ones. The philosophical debate uses words like heteronomy and autonomy, but many Jews have absorbed that perspective regardless of the terminology. This instinctive preference for personal input creates some tension when we understand the religion to merely want us to follow God's laws.[1]

I won't review the history of attempts to defend Judaism

---

1. That explains, for example, our discomfort with the *halachic* principle

against Kant's claims; I will only note that I hope to contribute to the discussion by showing he was wrong on both counts. Judaism is not as heteronomous as he assumed; most of my thrust will be to show that God "prefers" many free-willed human choices. On the other hand, we will repeatedly see why commandments would be a necessary aid to knowing how to make those decisions.

It Is Good That You Hold on to This, and also from This Rest not Your Hand

I am claiming, in other words, that I can stress both obedience to *halachah* and the importance of personal choice within a fully traditional religious view, and that doing so will materially advance our understanding of Judaism's message (for all humanity).

As in the first part, I am working my way towards very practical results. I do not want this to be a work of theory or intellectual interest; I want it to be the basis of seeing ways in which many observant Jews and Jewish communities need to recalibrate how we conduct our relationship with God, in ways that will give us a more productive, more positive experience of that relationship.

One difference from the first part is that here I will strive only to be persuasive, not unequivocal. In line with my stress on personal intuition, this section is more focused on my own insights, and I must therefore relinquish my attempts to be indisputable. The understandings of texts I will offer will be my best attempt to understand their intent, but I cannot say they are the only possible ways to read them.

I should note up front that some sources might seem to stress the opposite of what I am saying. Perhaps most famously, Jewish tradition took pride in the Jews' response to Moshe's asking them if they would accept the Torah, "We will do and we will

---

that גדול המצווה ועושה משאינו מצווה ועושה, that a commanded person who performs a deed is better or greater than one who does so voluntarily.

comprehend." As many sources note, the locution places obedience before understanding, chronologically and conceptually.[2]

I could try to collate all such sources and explain how they can be read in line with the theory I advance here, but the project would be long and tedious. The history of Jewish commentary shows, I think, that the gates of creativity are never shut or, as R. Matityahu haYizhari would have said it in the fifteenth century, when we say that God renews Creation daily in His goodness (המחדש בטובו בכל יום תמיד מעשה בראשית), that includes the ability to find new ideas in well-thumbed texts. Suffice it to say that I believe I could interpret each of the challenging texts in ways that would accord with my perspective, but consciously choose to focus on those sources that most clearly support my view.

Nor do I wish to pretend that what I am offering here is groundbreaking or revolutionary. While I believe we have fallen out of the habit of thinking this way, I claim that this awareness of the value of personal religious creativity has always been known. It was to rejuvenate that awareness in terms of the study and experience of *halachah* itself, I believe, that R. Joseph B. Soloveitchik, ob"m, wrote *Halachic Man* and *Halachic Mind*.

The Necessity and Role of *Halachah*

I believe R. Soloveitchik left room to explore further specifically on the question of commandedness. One side of that question wonders why God, Who values human intuition, commanded *mitzvot* at all. As part of my answer, I will try to show that God's original plan indeed envisioned a more minimal legal territory than currently, that God did "prefer" human autonomy in figuring out how best to serve Him.

The rules we have today, I adduce sources to suggest, only came about when humanity failed to come up with reasonable options of its own. God legislates where humanity was either unable or unwilling to understand the task ahead, failed to

---

2. See *Shabbat* 88a–b; R. Yonah Gerondi, *Sha`arei Teshuvah* II:10.

shoulder its responsibility to build a life of service based on the information at hand.

It is to make that argument most fully that I have chosen to order this part of the book chronologically, showing how God originally expected all people to figure out how to best serve Him, and then expected the same from Avraham and his descendants, only at the end coming to the world of *mitzvot* and the use of intuition it requires.

But if rules were God's way of reminding us of basic values we failed to understand on our own, some might assume we could return to making our own rules once we understood those values. If the original plan accepted or sought our creative input on how to serve God, some look to return to such a system today.

The error lies in losing sight of time's arrow; the job of each generation is to further the world we were bequeathed, not to try to create it anew. Born into a world where God has legislated, we can note the lost autonomy such legislation demonstrates, but we have no ability to turn the clock back to before that legislation had been promulgated. The Word, once given, lasts for the rest of eternity.

Confronting the Infinite

Yet it seems clear that God always intended to legislate *some* rules, even if only the one to desist from eating from the Tree of Knowledge. Aside from why that should be, we might easily also wonder why the response to human failures to observe a set of rules would be to give them *more* rules.

The answer to those questions, I think, lies in fully registering a fact Kant failed to take into account. He assumed human intuition and intellect can fully understand how to structure our lives. But religion plays in the garden of the Infinite, in the attempt to worship and become more similar to a God Who is so Other that we cannot possibly understand that God, or even just the best path to closeness to that God. Where we fail, either by not legislating properly or by not following those rules we already have, we identify a place where we need help, and God responds by laying out the path more fully.

A brief detour will help show why this would be. Frequently, we speak of God as infinite, and the way mathematicians dealt with the transfinite offers a good parallel for how I am suggesting *halachah* works. For much of human history, people shied away from the infinite itself; Aristotle famously denied the possibility of an actual infinity in the world, and his view held sway for millenia.

Only in the nineteenth century was a reasonable understanding of the infinite achieved, and then only by walling off their studies from any real-world parallels. Mathematicians had to leave their intuition behind because the infinite works nonintuitively or even counterintuitively, such as in the fact that adding to a transfinite set, even a huge amount, even another transfinite set — such as adding the odd numbers to the even numbers — does not change the set's size, since all three sets are still infinite.

And yet, again counterintuitively, some infinities are larger than others, as Georg Cantor, one of the early and most important students of the topic, demonstrated.[3]

Mathematicians' work on the transfinite offers a productive parallel to people's work to try to relate to God, the Infinite.[4] As in transfinite math, ordinary intuition must be trained before it can

---

3. Cantor's proof showed that in trying to match irrational decimals to the integers, there will always be an irrational decimal missing from the list. That is, Cantor showed that he could always construct a missing decimal from any such list. He did so by noting that each decimal would have as many digits as the number of the integer to which it was corresponding; by checking the value of that place within the decimal, Cantor said, he could say that *his* missing decimal would have a different value. This would mean that his constructed decimal would differ from every decimal on the list at at least one place; no matter how far down our list we would go, our decimal will differ from the nth one on the list at the nth spot.

4. David Foster Wallace, *Everything and More*, notes that Cantor saw his mathematical studies in just such religious terms.

define any correct forms of service of an Infinite Being (including how to handle many ordinary moral situations).

Similar to how the human mind needs workable rules, however strange, to avoid boggling in confronting a mathematical infinite, we need rules for how to relate to God. Some of those were given by God; some came later, but all were intended to ready us for autonomous activity once we had absorbed the thrust and intent of those rules.

Did Ramban Already Say This?

I believe this has all been said before, but mostly implicitly, leaving me the room to make it explicit. However, two well-known comments of Ramban, the thirteenth-century Spanish scholar, might lead some to assume this idea is so obvious and well-known as to make my writing superfluous.

Commenting on the Torah's commands קדושים תהיו and ועשית הישר והטוב, "You shall be holy" and "You shall do the right and the good,"[5] Ramban clearly calls for action that goes beyond the letter of the law. If we were sure that "going beyond" means creatively shaping our personal religiosity, my words here would be superfluous.

A closer look reveals that Ramban's position is not so clear. In the first comment, he says that the laws of the Torah do not necessarily prevent a person from being enslaved to such baser instincts as eating or sexual relations. To counterbalance that, he says, the Torah issues a general command to "be holy," to make clear that one cannot be satisfied with adherence to the letter of the law.

It is the insufficiency of law to fully determine good conduct that he is stressing, as we see in the second of those comments, where he adds:

וזה ענין גדול, לפי שאי אפשר להזכיר בתורה כל הנהגות האדם עם שכניו

---

5. *Vayikra* 19:2 and *Devarim* 6:18, with Ramban's comments there.

רעיו וכל משאו ומתנו ותקוני הישוב והמדינות כלם, אבל אחרי שהזכיר
מהם הרבה, כגון לא תלך רכיל (ויקרא יט טז), לא תקום ולא תטור (שם
פסוק יח)... וכיוצא בהן, חזר לומר בדרך כלל שיעשה הטוב והישר בכל
דבר, עד שיכנס בזה הפשרה ולפנים משורת הדין, וכגון מה שהזכירו בדינא
דבר מצרא (ב"מ קח א)...

And this is a great matter, because it is impossible to
mention in the Torah all of the ways in which a person
conducts himself with his neighbors and friends, and all
of his business dealings, and the way to set up society and
states in the best way; instead, after mentioning many of
them, such as "you shall not go talebearing," "do not take
vengeance or hold a grudge," ...and similar ones, it went
back to say generally that one should act well and good
in all matters, to the point that the person will, because
of this principle, compromise and act supererogatorily,
as the Talmud mentioned in the rules of *bar metsra*...[6]

Ramban *could* be making my point, that the Torah gives examples
from which we are supposed to extrapolate in building a life lived
in relation to God, but he equally might be assuming that we have
some kind of innate intuition as to what constitutes goodness or
even sanctity and sees these verses as appealing to that sense.[7]
If so, these comments say only that the Torah could not list all
that we know to be right and good, so it threw in a couple of
catchalls to remind us to follow those rules as well. That version
of Ramban's view says much less than I seek here.

---

6. The Talmudic principle that a person must give his neighbor the right
to buy his property before selling it to others.
7. Strikingly, Ramban's examples are hardly intuitive, although people
assume he meant them that way. Human insight does not naturally
reject gossip, does not see saving another's life as an absolute obligation, and does not even fully accept the wrong in holding a grudge. We
cannot know whether Ramban chose these examples to make that point
or these were just the ones that came to mind as he wrote.

One More Way of Thinking About It

There is a scientific concept that seems to me remarkably similar to how I will try to portray the balance between what God tells us and what we are supposed to get on our own, that of the complex adaptive system (CAS). Kevin Dooley explains:

> A CAS behaves/evolves according to three key prin-ciples: order is *emergent* as opposed to predetermined, the system's history is *irreversible*, and the system's future is often *unpredictable*. The basic building blocks of the CAS are *agents*. Agents are semi-autonomous units that seek to maximize some measure of goodness, or fitness, by evolving over time. Agents scan their environment and develop schema representing interpretive and action rules.[8]

Substitute "the nature of service of God" for Dooley's reference to "system," "Torah and *mitzvot*" for "environment," and "people" for "agents," and you get a good description of the kind of world I understand God to have been setting up. Torah, I will be suggest-ing, sets an environment that is emergent as opposed to prede-termined; is irreversible, so that we cannot bypass the history of *halachah* to get back to a previous time we'd prefer; and in which we cannot fully predict the direction the world will take.

By immersing themselves in the "environment," Torah, people elicit feedback as to the definition of service of God, with that feedback then shaping their future actions in a never-ending search for goodness, drawing them ever closer to God. Our abso-lute dependence on that feedback in improving our fitness is the piece Kant failed to see.

Or so I hope to show. I will begin with the time before the

---

8. Complex Adaptive Systems: A Nominal Definition, *http://www.eas.asu. edu/~KDooley/casopdef.html*, emphasis added. Dooley acknowledges earlier work by numerous scientists, including Murray Gell-Mann, in whose *The Quark and the Jaguar* (New York: Freedman & Co., 1994) I first encountered the concept.

Torah was given, before there was an identifiable Jewish people, to show that even then, as the Talmud presents it, God expected humanity to recognize their need to work to be more God-like. This is important for my central thesis, that God values human intuition, but also as a corrective to the sometime assumption that the Torah is largely indifferent to non-Jews and their spiritual health. In two ways, then, it is a productive first example of the Sages signaling that it has always been our failure to use our autonomy properly that leads God to make rules.

Chapter 13

The Case of the Noahides

Some of the derogatory Talmudic statements about non-Jews might give the impression that Judaism sees them as a lost cause. Perhaps adding to that, many have assumed that the commandments Judaism does apply to non-Jews are universally rational, meaning that the religion only asks them to adhere to a basic morality that is and should be obvious to everyone.

In the rest of this chapter, I offer evidence that the Talmud thought Scripture blamed non-Jews precisely for failing to realize that they were expected to figure out how to worship God on their own and were given commandments, known as the Noahide laws, only when they failed to do so. I will then show that the laws God gave them are not nearly as obvious, universal, or eminently rational as they are made out to be, that the laws in fact impose a vision of goodness and service of God that is far from intuitive or obvious.

Loosing the Bonds of the Nations: A Verse and Its Ramifications

Before I cite the Talmudic statement that anchors my argument, I want to note ahead of time that it sounds *aggadic*, like many other homiletic statements, and might therefore seem unable to bear the weight I will place on it (as I have noted, *aggadic* statements have to be used with great care). In this case, though, the statement comes as part of a series of inferences from a single verse, and several of those inferences carry *halachic* weight meant to be exercised in practice.

The Talmud is interpreting a verse in *Habakkuk*, "He stood

and measured the earth; he looked and shook the nations; then the eternal mountains were scattered, the everlasting hills sank low; his ways were as of old."[1] Commentators understood the text to refer to punishments administered to the generation of the Flood or of the Tower of Babel, but the Talmud sees it as revealing that non-Jews' failure to observe the Noahide laws led to their being punished in everlasting ways.[2]

Most of the examples the Talmud gives involve the loss of certain protections of law. For one example, the Talmud assumed that a Jew is not required to pay if his or her ox gores that of an idolatrous non-Jew. That is obviously a fraught position that would necessitate much discussion to fully explain, but is not my issue now; I raise it only as a reminder that the Talmud was in the midst of a *halachic*, not *aggadic*, conversation.

In that series of punishments, the last one asserts that the reference to God's having "loosed the bonds" refers in some way to the Noahide commandments. At first glance, this sounds like God absolved non-Jews of the need to follow those commandments (loosing those bonds); the Talmud rejects that possibility, since it would mean God had rewarded evildoers for their rebellion.

Instead, the Talmud suggests non-Jews are still obligated, but God rescinded the reward for following them. That fails as well, since it contradicts the accepted truth that non-Jews receive *great* reward for keeping those laws that apply to them. The Talmud therefore concludes that non-Jews only get reward as if they were performing these acts voluntarily, not the greater reward given to those who respond obediently to a command.

The give-and-take can be distracting, but in sum the Talmud reads the verse as meaning that non-Jews' failure to observe the Noahide laws left them with the lower reward given to those who voluntarily undertake a positive practice. And yet the Talmud and later authorities still assume that a non-Jew who specifically and formally recognizes that God commanded those observances

---

1. *Habakkuk* 3:6.
2. *Bava Kamma* 38a and *Avodah Zarah* 2b.

returns to the state of being rewarded as if commanded, a prime example being R. Meir's claim that a non-Jew involved with Torah receives reward like a High Priest.

The Elusive Commandment of Noahide Obligations

The Talmudic discussion is not yet comprehensible, though. First, it does not tell us the timing — when did God command the Noahide laws, and when did He punish them for their failure to fulfill them? Second, if God did decide to punish non-Jews, why in such a minimal way, a loss of a level of reward, which, incidentally, would matter little to non-Jews who had already demonstrated their indifference to these laws.

Adding to the confusion, the Talmud presents a mixed message when it refers to God's giving the Noahide laws: sometimes it refers to command,[3] but other times speaks of non-Jews having *accepted* the laws upon themselves,[4] which suggests voluntary adherence. Perhaps most interestingly, the Talmud interchanges the terms on occasion,[5] as if there were no significant difference, although we have just seen one.

The Scriptural source for these laws does little to clear up the matter.[6] The Talmud points to the verse, "And the Lord God commanded the man saying, From all the trees of the Garden you may freely eat.[7] Noting that the words of this verse, elsewhere in Scripture, refer to the laws of idolatry, blasphemy, establishing a

---

3. Tosefta *Sotah* 6:9, *Avodah Zarah* 7:4, and *Sanhedrin* 74b refers only to their having been commanded.
4. See, for example, *Avodah Zarah* 2b and 64b, where the Sages require a *ger toshav*, a resident alien, to formally accept the seven commandments that the Noahides accepted. This example is particularly interesting, since it is in the context of requiring the non-Jew to repeat an earlier commitment, yet refers to that original commitment as having been self-initiated.
5. *Bava Kamma* 38a and *Sanhedrin* 56a-b.
6. *Sanhedrin* 56b.
7. *Bereshit* 2:16.

court system, prohibiting murder, incest, theft, and the eating of limbs from live animals, the Talmud assumes those same words in this verse mean them as well.

For just one example of how this works, the word "commanded" (in the phrase "And the Lord God commanded") is taken to refer to the requirement to establish a court system, because another verse in Genesis uses the same verb when referring to Avraham's ordering his children and descendants to act justly. Since courts are venues of justice, "commanded" indicates issues of justice.

The technique is commonplace in Talmudic literature but startling here, because it seems to assume that *Adam and his descendants* would have understood God's words to them according to their meaning elsewhere in Scripture (which had not yet been revealed to humanity). As if he were alert to this problem, Rambam formulates the commanding of the Noahide laws in a notably convoluted way:

> Adam was commanded about six matters, idolatry, blasphemy…and courts; even though all of these are a tradition in our hands from Moshe our teacher and the intellect inclines towards them, from the general tenor of the words of the Torah it appears he was commanded about these.[8]

Rambam could have said that God commanded six rules; instead, he recognizes the authoritative tradition that these were commanded, notes that they are the kinds of obligations towards which the intellect inclines (which, I will claim, is not the same as saying they are fully intuitive), and grudgingly concedes that the "general tenor" of the Torah's words *could* mean Adam was

---

8. *Hilchot Melachim* 9:1. There are only six because Rambam accepted another Talmudic tradition that eating meat was prohibited until after the Flood, so the commandment of *ever min ha-hay*, eating a piece of an animal that was removed in the animal's lifetime, could not have come until then.

expected to observe them. He does not explain why he said it this way, but the obscurity of the Talmudic derivation seems a likely candidate.

In his reference to these being the kinds of acts towards which our intellects incline, Rambam obliquely reminds us to wonder why God felt the need to command propositions and modes of behavior that were intellectually obvious. Although Rambam does not to my knowledge say this, R. Nissim of Kairouan, a tenth-century North African scholar, took for granted that non-Jews are obligated to fulfill *any* intuitive responsibility, his specific example being the need to honor parents.[9]

Rambam would likely have known R. Nissim's work, but not that of Rashbam, a twelfth-century biblical and Talmudic commentator, who made a similar assumption when reading a verse that speaks of Avraham having observed God's Torah. The verse is difficult, since both Torah and the commandments had yet to be given. Rashbam assumes Avraham observed all the commandments the human intellect can come to on its own; indeed, he went further, arguing these are fully in force even absent a divine command. Some of Rashbam's examples are Noahide laws, but others are not, such as welcoming guests.[10]

Could Rationally Obvious Ideas Be Considered Commanded?

All of these oddities make sense if we assume that, at least until the time of the Flood, people were both privileged and required to define their obligations to God on their own.[11] That is not true

---

9. Introduction to the Talmud, printed in the Rom Talmud. R. Nissim further assumed that *Hullin* 92a's reference to 30 commandments that Noahides accepted meant ones they intuited *before* the giving of the Torah at Sinai. The Talmud does not list the 30, but others have tried to reconstruct it, notably Samuel b. Hofni Gaon of the tenth century and R. Menahem Azariah da Fano of the sixteenth century.

10. Rashbam, *Bereshit*, 26:5, s.v. *Hukkotai*.

11. That also seems to be Rambam's assumption in the *Guide* II:39, where

of the Noahide laws the Talmud defines, since elements of those were decidedly *not* universally intuitive, as we will see next chapter. Rather, I am suggesting that had human beings shouldered their responsibility correctly, God might have been equally satisfied with a similar but not identical set of laws.

That explains the prooftext the Talmud offers, in which the literal sense says that God permitted all the trees in the Garden but one, and the Talmud showed how each word echoes another in Scripture. Perhaps the statement was indeed meant to be filled with meaning, each word symbolizing a mode of behavior, but that it was originally *Adam*'s right and obligation to articulate that meaning.

After the Flood, God defined them more exactly, and we could never go back. But before the Flood, perhaps, the command was fluid enough that it could also have encompassed other visions of law. It is that fluidity, perhaps, that Rambam was noting when he spoke of the "general tenor" of the Torah's words.

Humanity's failure to flesh out a life of morality and striving to get closer to the Creator finally "forced" God to punish the generations of the Flood or the Tower, as mentioned in *Habakkuk*. If so, the punishment was not for specific transgressions, it was for the failure to articulate and adhere to a reasonable standard of behavior.

This would mean that before the event referenced in *Habakkuk*, a non-Jew who behaved morally out of a belief in a God who desires moral behavior would have been rewarded as if he had observed a *commandment*, a specific order from God to act this way. Thus, for R. Nissim of Kairouan, for example, a non-Jew who honored a parent — despite there having been no specific command to do so — would have been rewarded by God as if he or she were responding properly to a Divine dictate.

---

he asserts that only Moshe's prophecy produced legislation.

A First Example of Autonomy Lost

That is not the state of Noahide law in Jewish thought since at least Talmudic times. Rambam famously writes that non-Jews who keep the Noahide laws are considered of the "righteous of the nations" and earn a share in the World to Come *only* if they accept those obligations because God commanded them in the Torah. I am suggesting that that became true after the time of the Divine decision reflected in *Habakkuk*, when God limited their right of autonomous legislation.

Ramban, too, differentiates an ordinary moral non-Jew from a *ger toshav*, a resident alien, along these lines. Though their actions may be exactly the same, the former is rewarded as a volunteer while the latter as one commanded, precisely because he has formally agreed to observe the Jewish vision and version of the Noahide laws.[12]

To my mind, then, the Talmud reads the verse in *Habakkuk* as indicating a significant shift in God's relationship to humanity, somewhere around the time of the Flood or the Tower of Babel. Originally, God wanted humans to articulate or create their own morality, as long as it fit the one explicit command not to eat from the Tree of Knowledge of Good and Evil.

When we failed at that task, God required us to accept and adhere to predetermined laws, a first instance where the descent into heteronomy starts with the failure to properly handle the responsibility of autonomy. Even so, these commandments are not so restrictive as to prevent creative human input. Rather, they inculcate a worldview that is supposed to form the basis of independent and personal contributions to the world, as I will show.

---

12. Novellae to *Makkot* 9a.

Chapter 14

The Worldview of the Noahide Laws: Far From Intuitive

Last chapter, I understood the Talmud to indicate God originally wanted and expected human beings to define right and
wrong themselves, which would have created a reasonable alternative to the Noahide laws that were eventually ordained. Even
after those laws were legislated, I now want to show, they function
differently than people often assume.

Some scholars, for example, claim that the Noahide laws were
really a way for Jews to govern the non-Jews who lived among
them.[1] While these laws are certainly also that, they are not only
that, since the Talmud sees them as applying to all non-Jews
wherever they live. More accurately, then, these laws articulate
the minimal requirements God set for humanity.[2]

A second segment of thinkers cite some Talmudic texts to
support their view that Noahide laws are really just expressions

---

1. Of course, a Jewish state run according to *halachah* would require adherence to those laws by any non-Jews who wished to reside among them;
   see Rambam, *Book of the Commandments*, Prohibition 51 and *Hilchot
   Avodah Zarah* 10:6. The idea starts with Hugo Grotius, who called
   them a Jewish version of *ius gentium*, laws the Romans promulgated
   to govern their relationships with non-Romans. On this, see Alasdair
   MacIntyre, *Whose Justice? Which Rationality?* (U. of Notre Dame: Notre
   Dame, 1988), p. 149. For my own ideas about how Noahide law could
   serve as a useful model of alienage law for the U.S., see my "Involuntary
   Particularism: The Noahide Laws, Citizenship, and Alienage," 18 *Geo.
   Immigr. L.J.* 543.
2. This also might explain why Judaism saw each of these as capital crimes
   — they were defining the absolute minimum of what it means to be
   human, so that violating them forfeits one's right to life.

of principles any rational human being would have to accept, Divine command or no.[3] The late Prof. Marvin Fox, among others, disagreed.[4] He argued that the Talmud only meant that we could explain these laws in a way that made sense to outsiders, not that we would have figured them out ourselves. Central to his view was Rambam's ruling that non-Jews only earn a share in the World to Come if they keep these *mitzvot* because of God's having

---

3. For a discussion of Moses Mendelssohn, Hermann Cohen, and other similar thinkers, see the relevant chapters in David Novak, *The Image of the Non-Jew in Judaism: An Historical and Constructive Study of the Noahide Laws* (New York: Edwin Mellen, 1983). Novak offers his own views in *Natural Law in Judaism* (Cambridge: Cambridge U. Press, 1998). See also Nahum Rakover's "Jewish Law and the Noahide Obligation to Preserve Social Order," *Cardozo Law Review* 12 (1991):1073–1136 and *Law and the Noahides: Law as a Universal Value* (Jerusalem, 1998), a translation of his Hebrew book on the topic.

   Two Talmudic discussions come closest to portraying Noahide laws as natural, but each has significant problems: 1) *Eruvin* 100b states that without revelation, humans still would have learned modesty from the cat, thrift from the ant, incest from the dove, and sexual etiquette from the rooster. Even were we to grant that this meant people would have inferred a *religious* obligation to be modest, etc., Noahide laws do not deal with all of those, and in some cases, expect a lot more than we would have gotten from the animals. 2) The second source, *Yoma* 67b, defines *mishpatim*, one of the words the Bible uses for laws, as rules worthy of being promulgated even had the Torah not done so. The simplest interpretation of that statement is that these laws are so intuitive as to be part of every society's legal system, especially as *mishpatim* are being contrasted to *hukim*, laws outsiders attack as senseless. Five of the examples given are also in the Noahide list, suggesting they are, indeed, universally intuitive. As we will see, though, there are two others on the Noahide list, the obligation to set up a legal system and the prohibition against eating a limb cut off of a living animal, and the details of the other five — as I discuss — should make it clear that the Talmud at most meant the outlines of these laws were intuitive, but not their full content.

4. Marvin Fox, "Rambam and Aquinas on Natural Law," *Dine Israel* 3 (1972), pp. 10 and 26. See also J. David Bleich, "Judaism and Natural Law," *Jewish Law Annual* VII (1988), 5–42.

commanded them.[5] If Rambam insists on an awareness of divine command, whether or not these laws are obvious is apparently irrelevant.

A Third Way: Noahide Law That Assumes Natural Morality

My teacher and master, R. Aharon Lichtenstein of Yeshivat Har Etzion,[6] offers a middle view. R. Lichtenstein says Judaism certainly assumes a natural morality, intuitive and universally binding on all human beings.[7] That morality, however, is not the same as Noahide law, a point also made by R. Dr. Norman Lamm and Prof. Aaron Kirschenbaum.[8]

This important distinction means that despite the existence of an intuitive and universal human morality — perhaps the kind that R. Nissim and Rashbam assumed was always obligatory, as we saw in the previous chapter — God decided (or was forced by human failure) to legislate more specifically. My point here is that those specific laws inculcate a worldview, not just a broad morality everyone would agree to anyway. At the same time, we will see that God still left significant freedom for human input into defining the good life.

The Noahide laws[9] obligate people to: build a society, not just

---

5. *Hilchot Melachim* 8:11.

6. Not to be confused with Aaron Lichtenstein, author of *Seven Laws of Noah* (New York: RJJ, 1986), who also figures in discussions of Noahide law.

7. R. Aharon Lichtenstein, "Does Jewish Tradition Recognize An Ethic Independent of Halachah?" *Modern Jewish Ethics* (Ohio State, 1975), 62–4.

8. A. Kirschenbaum and N. Lamm, "Freedom and Constraint in the Jewish Judicial Process," *Cardozo Law Review* 1 (Spring, 1979), p. 120ff. See also J. David Bleich, "Judaism and Natural Law," pp. 13–25.

9. This was true at least from the time of the Talmudic traditions about those laws; I leave open the possibility, as I noted in the previous chapter, that the original Noahide laws were open to various definitions, especially since some of the *halachah* to which the Talmud relates those

see themselves as a concatenation of individuals who happen to live near each other; submit themselves, in heart and mind, to the One God; *strictly* respect life and property rights; express their sexuality away from their family of origin and only in relationships that could theoretically produce offspring; and to recognize that animals only become food after they have died.

These were, I contend, the basic building blocks God wanted of any human society; from there, societies were free to move in multiple directions, as long as they did not lose sight of those basics. Only by discussing each of those laws, however, can we fully see the extent to which they both imposed a particular view of the world and left room for individual and national input into the definition of goodness.

Dinin — The Social System

While the Talmud is clear that non-Jews are obligated to establish courts, it does not further define the obligation. The later writers who discuss it agree the courts must do more than just stop or avoid conflict, and seem to me to see the law to require each society to establish a shared vision of social structure and ideals.

Rambam, the earliest of the three best-known contributors to the topic, justified Shimon and Levi's killing the people of Shechem[10] by saying that the citizens of Shechem were capitally liable for their failure to judge or punish the prince who kidnapped Dinah.[11] This solves the theological problem of how

---

laws had itself not yet been given. This would depend on the extent to which we believe that Talmudic references to Torah's always existing and to the Patriarchs having kept all of *halachah* are meant literally, or in terms of broad ideals and worldview, itself a debated topic that I leave for another time.

10. *Bereshit* 34.

11. At the same time, Rambam does not require Noahides to sacrifice their lives to fulfill this precept; see *Hilchot Melachim* 10:2. If so, Rambam assumes Shechem did not have the power to impose his will on the people, which then raises the question of when Rambam would obligate

two of Yaacov's sons — progenitors of Tribes of Israel, deeply admired by Jewish tradition — could commit mass murder, but it also takes a position on individual and communal accountability for society's legal health. Rambam's assumption of extensive observer-responsibility is certainly not universally obvious, since current Western morality sees such bystander involvement as meritorious but not obligatory.

In addition, Ramban disagreed, which means Rambam's idea is not obvious even to Jews. Ramban instead thinks that *dinin* mandates establishing a system of civil law. He did not set exact parameters for what this system had to cover, but gave numerous examples, including "theft, overcharging, withholding wages, bailments, rape and seduction, torts, lending, business, and so on."[12] In this reading, the non-Jewish obligation was primarily to set up a functioning legal system, including courts. Incidentally, he saw all this as a positive requirement rather than a capital crime.

Ramban does not mention how he expects non-Jews to arrive at their laws, which would seem to leave the process up to them. If so, he is assuming that members of each society must band together at least enough to agree on a set of rules governing their conduct, which necessarily involves decisions about that society's character and ideals.

R. Moshe Isserles, the sixteenth-century codifier of Jewish law known as Rema, understood Ramban to have gone a step further; Rema thought non-Jewish courts were required to adopt *Jewish law* in these areas.[13] Jewish civil law is not only not universally intuitive, it conveys very pointed moral and spiritual lessons

---

non-Jews to protest a corrupt system or leader and when he would concede that circumstances exempted them from that.

12. Commentary on *Bereshit* 34:13.

13. *Responsa Rema* 10. *Responsa Hatam Sofer* 6:14 and *Responsa Tsits Eliezer* 16:55 analyze Rema's view at length; R. Sofer at least seems to accept it. R. Naftali Zevi Yehudah Berlin (Netsiv), *Haamek She'alah* 3:2 disagreed, citing *Psalms* 147:20 — "He has not done so to any nation, nor has he informed them of laws [*mishpatim*]" — as proof that Jewish civil law was given only to Jews.

about how to handle business and social dealings. For Rema, Noahides need to adopt that value system in their civil law.

Whichever of the interpretations we adopt, *dinin* pushes for a society that shapes its citizens' lives and worldviews in more than minimal ways. Rema seems to have expected all human society to adopt the Jewish mode of handling civil matters, and Ramban at least required non-Jews to make decisions about those questions, which inherently involve deciding what kind of society to inhabit. Rambam's different approach still requires citizens to see society as a cooperative, cohesive venture, in which they police each other's conduct at least around their basic laws.

For the latter two, while the Noahide law of *dinin* imposes a significant obligation, and requires establishing a society in some broad sense, it leaves the character of that society largely up to its members. What is imposed is the need to care about society's rules and administration of justice; much of the rest is left up to them.

Idolatry Laws as an Introduction to Jewish Monotheism

In prohibiting idolatry, the Noahide laws again demand that non-Jews accept a fairly particular view of the world. The idolatry prohibition rules out accepting any power other than God as ruler of the universe; it is difficult to imagine that even Jews saw these commandments as intuitive,[14] since paganism was alive and well in the time of the Talmud — Christianity did not conquer the Roman world until the fourth century, and paganism survived in Persia well beyond then.

Too, traditional Jewish law counted at least some versions of

---

14. Rambam thought he could logically prove the existence of a single God. At the same time, in *Hilchot Avodah Zarah* 1:3, he assumes that Avraham spent thirty-seven years struggling with the issue before deciding that there was only one God.

major *modern* religions as idol-worshipping.[15] When the Talmud refers to idol worship as a prohibition that all understood, it can only have meant that non-Jews would understand monotheists' prohibiting idolatry, not that they would instantly accept that point of view.

Another element to this law in the Talmudic understanding is that it includes any bowing down, offering incense, sacrifice, or libation to a power other than God, even if the sects that serve those powers don't value those forms of worship. The Talmud notes that because these were central practices in the *Beit haMikdash*, the Jewish Temple, they count as worship whenever they are done.[16] Just expressing admiration or love for an idol does not incur the same penalty, but performing *avodot penim*, acts of worship that occurred within the sanctuary of the Temple itself, is instantly worthy of death penalty.[17]

I highlight this because it means that to fully understand the obligation to avoid idolatry, a non-Jew would need to learn about Judaism and its Temple. True, the non-Jew could avoid this by refraining from expressing any positive feelings for powers other than the Creator of the World, but that, too, means he has accepted Jewish monotheism.

---

15. An extensive literature discusses Jewish definitions of idolatry, too vast to analyze here. For some examples, Catholic views of the Trinity have been widely considered idolatrous, while many Protestant versions are not. Hinduism worships many gods, but some argue that those should be seen as avenues to, or expressions of, the one central god. Similarly, the apparent idolatry in bowing down to a statue of the Buddha is explained by some adherents as only enunciating respect for the life he lived and the ideals he taught. In each case, the Jewish view is at the very least not intuitive to millions of people, even after thousands of years of monotheistic rhetoric, supporting my claim that these laws were doing something more than ratifying well-accepted truths.

16. *Sanhedrin* 60b.

17. *Hilchot Melachim* 9:2, based on *Sanhedrin* 56b, which ties a Noahide's liability into a Jew's being killed by a court for his worship.

The Jewishness of the Laws of Blasphemy

The blasphemy laws also adopt a nonintuitive view of what constitutes rebellion against God. Simply saying, for example, "I hate God I hope He *x*," while not lauded, would not qualify as capital blasphemy. Instead, the Talmud limits the death penalty to where the blasphemer uses a name of God as part of the curse. In the Talmudic idiom, only saying "Yose should hit (or kill) Yose," with Yose being a euphemism for names of God, is a capital crime. Cursing God is legally meaningless unless the power invoked is the only Power that could conceivably affect that Being.

Full understanding of the laws of blasphemy also introduces Noahides to the esoteric matter of the Names of God. The Talmud assumes that the special name of God (YHWH; Rambam thinks the four-letter name that starts AD__ also qualifies)[18] and any *kinui*, reference name, would be a problem. Rambam thinks *kinui* includes: (1) names that are not among the seven special names of God, such as *Elokim* or *Tsevakot*, (2) the words for qualities Scripture attached to God, such as compassionate and merciful, and (3) other languages' terms for God, such as Allah, God, or Dieu.[19] There are other views as well, but they share in common the assumption that a non-Jew who wants to be sure to avoid blasphemy would have to learn about what Jews see as a Name of God.

The first three Noahide laws, then, show us that there is more going on here than a universal morality all right-thinking people would arrive at on their own. In teaching about building a society, the absolute necessity of belief in one God who is the sole power that runs the universe and about the need to treat that God with respect, they each show that a full definition of goodness only comes from understanding how Jews worship and refer to God,

---

18. *Sanhedrin* 56a and Rambam, *Hilchot Avodah Zarah* 2:7.
19. *Hilchot Shevuot* 2:2. Others seem to have limited capital liability to *Scriptural* names of God, such as *Elokim* or *Tsevaot*; see, e.g., Rashi to *Sanhedrin* 56a, s.v. *ve-aliba de-Rabi Meir*, who lists only actual names of God when he refers to *kinuim*.

while still leaving much room for personal shaping of a relationship with God.

Murder

Murder in its starkest form is perhaps the most intuitive crime around, but the Noahide code prohibits and punishes forms of the act that are today much debated. In Noahide law, for some examples, killing a person who is terminally ill (or wounded), a fetus, oneself, and even indirectly but premeditatedly causing another's death are all capital murder.[20] The vigorous debate about each of these issues in modern societies — abortion, assisted and ordinary suicide, and the level of liability for indirect killing — sufficiently proves that the Talmud's definition is not universally obvious.

More than that, these rules make a significant programmatic claim, that all human life, however underdeveloped or certain to expire, is off-limits to active intervention to end it. Again, a rule that might seem minimal teaches a specific perspective of an issue important to any society and one that is vigorously argued today.

Incest — Focusing Sexuality on Marriage and Childbearing

We often assume incest laws are intuitive, but, interestingly, Rambam and Ramban each struggle to explain the prohibitions.[21] For non-Jews, the problem is perhaps even harder, since the Talmudic definition does not follow any sort of inherently intuitive model. There is debate about the conclusions of that

---

20. For indirect killing, see *Hilchot Melachim* 9:4. Although not our issue here, I believe Rambam sees Jews' exemption from capital punishment in such cases as stemming from the belief that God will take care of those forms of the crime; see *Hilchot Rotseach* 2:2–4 and 3:10. That non-Jews cannot rely on Divine intervention seems to reflect a belief that Providence affects Jews more directly than others.
21. See Rambam, *Hilchot Melachim* 9:5–8 and Ramban, *Vayikra* 18:6.

discussion, but Rambam rules that the Noahide laws prohibit sexual relations for a man with his mother, his father's wife, married women, his maternal (but not paternal) half-sisters, other men, and animals.[22]

I suggest the Talmud's derivation also gives its underlying logic. Parsing the verse that first discusses human marriage — "Therefore shall a man leave his mother and father and cleave to his wife and they shall be one flesh"[23] — the Talmud infers that human sexuality must involve leaving one's parents (the father's wife stands in for the father himself) to create a physical interlocking (of the sort only men and women can create, not men and men)[24] with one's wife (and not a woman married to someone else), that will, in the ordinary course of events, lead them to become as one flesh (in the form of a baby), which rules out bestiality.

Sexuality, in this presentation, is an extension of marriage and childbearing; only those relationships that *could* be marital, of the *form* where the physical union could produce children, are allowed.[25] Once again, heteronomously imposed and yet, in

---

22. Rambam devotes significantly more space to incest and eating a limb cut off of a living animal than to the other Noahide laws, perhaps because these were least intuitive. Other medieval authorities such as R. Meir Abulafia, *Yad Ramah* to *Sanhedrin* 57b-58b, defined the incest prohibitions differently, but the overall principles seem to be the same.

23. *Bereshit* 2:24.

24. The prohibition of homosexuality was also not intuitive, in Talmudic times or our own; its inclusion in the Noahide laws is not what everyone of the time knew to be right; it is a corollary of the assumption that sexuality should relate to producing children.

25. I stress that this requirement is formal rather than practical. It is not that this man and this woman need to be able to have children — people beyond childbearing years can also marry — but that the physical act they engage in be one that could produce children. I would note, however, that the Biblical story of Sarah suggests, *inter alia*, that our knowledge that a woman can no longer give birth is not as absolute as we tend to assume. If so, relations between a man and a woman are always able to produce children, at least in theory.

defining proper human sexuality, leaving broad discretion to the Noahides.

Theft

Like murder, theft as a broad concept is intuitive, but its exact definition and the punishment accorded it in the Noahide code goes beyond the expected. First, Noahide law punishes theft of even minimal amounts of money, even if the victim is not the rightful owner. Second, like all Noahide law, theft is considered a capital crime. In the most extreme example, if one non-Jew steals a minimal amount of money and another steals it from him, Noahide law would call for both thieves to be put to death.[26]

The Talmud and later writers do not state it this way because they expected this outcome to be put into practice — the Talmud recorded these discussions hundreds of years after Jewish courts had the power to execute, especially when the defendant was non-Jewish — but to make a moral point. Theft in Noahide law is not primarily intended to protect owners, it is a way to stress the *absolute* inviolability of others' property. As we might say to a child, if it's not yours, don't take it. Obviously, however, that extreme reaction to even minimal theft is neither intuitive nor universally obvious.[27]

That the *halachah* prohibits a maternal half-sister but not a paternal one, *Hilchot Melachim* 9:5, removes genetics as our concern. The Talmud does not explain the distinction, but I suspect it has to do with the man having come out of the same womb as a maternal half-sister.

26. See *Hilchot Melachim* 9:9, based on *Avodah Zarah* 72a.
27. I suspect most of us find it difficult to justify the death penalty, even in theory, for stealing a few dollars. That may reveal how inured we have become to theft's ubiquity; were we more sensitive to the damage theft does to a social sense of unity and common purpose, we might understand better how it could arouse the kind of moral revulsion usually reserved for murder or rape — which, incidentally, is seen as a kind of theft by at least one rabbinic author.

Ever Min haHay — The Limbs of a Living Animal

Many who study Noahide law assume that the prohibition against eating parts taken off a living animal is a safeguard against cruelty.[28] That already gives the commandment an educative component, although perhaps one we would see as obvious.

Two details suggest the law is actually focused elsewhere. First, the prohibition applies to *eating* such pieces of animals, not *removing* them. Second, the law does not care *how* the limb was removed; a limb amputated under full sedation and for the animal's health is just as prohibited as one torn off cruelly.

It seems to me, therefore, that the prohibition is actually concerned with stressing that animal flesh cannot be thought of as food while the animal is still alive. The Talmud assumes that God only first permitted animal flesh after the Flood;[29] the prohibition of אבר מן החי makes it capitally clear that that permission only starts after death. And yet, while that specific point is mandated, it leaves much room for deciding how to make use of the animal kingdom in one's eating needs.

Cross-Breeding — A Simple Prohibition

I think I have already shown that Noahide laws do more than articulate obvious and universal ideas about how to live a good human life. Fundamental (and nonobvious) Jewish ideas about how to relate to God, to sex, to others' lives and property, and to food are all incorporated here; non-Jews need not become Jews, but they are expected to accept core Jewish beliefs about the proper conduct of the world and human society.

A lesser-known aspect of the Noahide code is that it is not limited to the seven capital crimes. There are several opinions

---

28. Aaron Lichtenstein, *The Seven Laws of Noah*, 2nd ed. (New York: RJJ School, 1986), p. 56 mentions the cruelty aspect but also gives the suggestion I give in the text, that it helps define food.
29. *Sanhedrin* 59b. A similar stress on reminding humans of the seriousness of eating animals might underlie the *kashrut* rules given to Jews.

in the Talmud about which prohibitions do and do not apply, but Rambam, at least, understood the Talmud to include grafting fruit from one type of tree to another or mating animals of different species — cross-breeding — as simple Noahide prohibitions. Jewish thinkers commonly understand that prohibition, for Jews, as teaching us to see the sufficiency of God's Creation, a lesson we could imagine God wanting non-Jews to learn as well.[30]

Loosely Defined Obligations — Reminders of Continuing Autonomy

Tradition also assumed that non-Jews bore responsibilities to the world, to others, and to God; we will take an example of each. First, the Mishnah assumes a general human obligation to populate and inhabit the world, based on the verse in *Isaiah* 45:18, "not for chaos did He create it, to be inhabited He formed it."

The explicit discussion focused on sexual relationships, but *Beit Shammai's* locution, "the world was only created for procreation," convinced numerous Jewish scholars that non-Jews, too, are obligated to bear children.[31] If so, the verse would seem to extend to more than just *having* those children, but ensuring that the world they inherit is one that can be well-inhabited.[32] This at

---

30. *Hilchot Melachim* 10:6; for the reason, see *Sefer haChinuch, Mitzvah* 244. That the rule is limited to trees and animals, where Jews could not crossbreed plants either, suggests that the *visibility* of the crossbreeding was the central problem. What that would mean for various industries today is an interesting *halachic* discussion worthy of further thought in another venue.

31. See, for some examples, *Sheiltot R. Ahai Gaon, Sheilta* 165, *Tosafot Hagigah* 2b, s.v. *Lo*. Two important commentators on R. Joseph Caro's *Shulchan Aruch* (Code of Jewish Law), *Beit Shemuel* and *Magen Avraham*, similarly assumed a general human obligation to marry (or cohabit) and bear children; see their comments to *Even haEzer* 1 and *Orah Hayyim* 146 respectively.

32. This also reflects God's original desire, in *Bereshit*, to put humans into the Garden "to work it and preserve it," as R. Aharon Lichtenstein has noted in public lectures.

least implies raising children to be productive adults, acting with an eye towards ecological responsibility (however we define that), and quite possibly urges some level of political involvement.

Here, we have a good example of a legislated obligation that still demands personal and nonobvious choices as to how to fulfill it. Aside from how many children to have and when, there are numerous good and important ways to contribute to ensuring that God's world does not descend into chaos, and nothing in the obligation tells us which of those paths to take. It's a necessary personal choice.

Charity

Noting a verse where God speaks of Avraham commanding all his descendants to perform righteousness and justice in the land, the Talmud assumes that non-Jews are required to give charity.[33] While Avraham's male descendants might be obligated only to set up courts, women's "righteousness" had to mean acts of charity. We will come back to charity in Jewish contexts, but a first point is that there is no unequivocal definition of what charity to perform when; it takes personal choices.

Prayer

R. Moshe Feinstein ob"m, the leading rabbinic decisor of the late twentieth century, assumed the obligation to pray was an extension of the obligation to believe in God.[34] While there is room to disagree, those who accept his idea would presumably also see non-Jews as obligated to incorporate belief in God in other areas of their life as well, legislated or not.

---

33. *Sanhedrin* 57b, citing *Bereshit* 18:19. The exact derivation is not straightforward, but also not our issue. Note that the Talmud infers ideals of non-Jewish behavior from Avraham, meaning it sees him as an exemplary non-Jew, aside from his role as founder of the Jewish people.
34. *Responsa Iggerot Mosheh, Orah Hayyim* 2:28.

How Would They Know About This?

Perhaps the most perplexing aspect of the Noahide laws is that Judaism makes no explicit provision for communicating them. Unless God takes joy in others' continuing failure, there would have to be at least some way non-Jews could be expected to come to understand their obligations towards God and the world.

The Talmud's view of the respect non-Jews are mandated to show Jews[35] suggests an avenue. Cynics might see this Talmudic emphasis as an exercise in self-esteem, in seeing ourselves as superior to those around us. I believe, instead, that it was meant to lead non-Jews to ask how we see their responsibilities in life. While few non-Jews have thus far acknowledged Jews as the source of this vital information, the Talmud at least lets us see how the system expected or hoped non-Jews would learn how to live properly.

Acknowledging Jews' Otherness

First, the Sifre, an authoritative extra-Talmudic collection of legal inferences from Scripture, requires even גרי תושב, non-Jews who adhere to the Noahide laws, to live in separate cities within a Jewish commonwealth.[36] Since *halachah* entitles such non-Jews to the same social welfare benefits as Jews,[37] this cannot be an expression of disapproval. Rather, it articulates who owns the Land; these non-Jews are welcome outsiders, but not full members or citizens.

The Talmudic rhetoric about a non-Jew who hits a Jew, observes the Sabbath, or studies Torah, goes even further. The

---

35. In any discussion like this, I repeatedly stress that these differences are religious and not genetic or racial. Non-Jews are free to convert and enjoy the rights and responsibilities of Jewish life, such as they may be.

36. Sifre *Devarim* 259. Rabad, ibid., assumes that Rambam would maintain that rule even today, while he himself only draws that distinction when the Jewish commonwealth is fully functional.

37. See Rambam, *Hilchot Matnot Aniyim* 7:1 and Rabad's gloss to *Hilchot Issurei Biah* 14:8.

Talmudic metaphor has it that a non-Jew hitting a Jew is akin to that non-Jew doing so to God, as it were; for non-Jews, Jews are supposed to serve as physical representations of God, such that hitting a Jew is "like" hitting God. (Incidentally, for Jews, that same comparison comes up in terms of how to treat parents.)[38]

The Talmud sees the right to take a day a week to cease all productive activity as a special gift to the Jewish people; normal humans were supposed to be contributing daily to the settlement of the world.[39] Similarly, the study of Torah is seen as the vehicle of a unique bond between God and the Jewish people; a non-Jew who intrudes on that bond by studying Torah — other than to know how to act — deserves death, a phrase that, as I have noted before, expresses a value rather than a practical outcome.[40]

The World of *Mitzvot*

These examples of excluding non-Jews become more notice-able given that the religion generally welcomes non-Jewish

---

38. *Sanhedrin* 58b with Rambam, *Hilchot Melachim* 10:6. For parents, see *Sanhedrin* 50b.
39. Ibid., which derives the prohibition from *Bereshit* 8:22's reference to the world's functioning productively, "day or night." The rule sounds more onerous than it is, as Hatam Sofer (R. Moshe Sofer, 1762–1839), notes in his novellae on the tractate. He speaks of vacations specifically, but his point is that any productive activity — spending time with one's children, attending meetings for charitable causes, and demonstrating at political rallies — is also a way to contribute to the world's running. Medieval commentators such as Rashi, R. Meir haLevi Abulafia, and Rambam have slightly different versions of what exactly the non-Jew may not do.
40. *Sanhedrin* 59a. If we recall Rema's view that *dinin* included all of Jewish civil law, he would have to allow non-Jews to study all the topics and tractates that elucidate those laws, a huge chunk of the Talmudic corpus. Rather than caring about non-Jews gaining certain kinds of knowledge, the Talmud seems focused on prohibiting the act of Torah study as an independent religious experience.

performance of *mitzvot*.[41] For a surprising example, Rambam allows a Jew to circumcise a non-Jew, as long as the non-Jew intends the circumcision to fulfill the Biblical commandment.[42] I note that in particular because the Bible and Talmud stress the covenantal significance of circumcision.[43] Allowing non-Jews to perform the act without converting is an extreme example of the religion's openness to partial observance.[44]

Taken together with the requirement to live in separate cities and the harshness of the reaction towards a non-Jew assaulting a Jew, studying Torah, or keeping Shabbat, I understand these rules as expressing the system's hope that non-Jews would recognize Jewish exceptionalism and treat them accordingly, especially in turning to them for guidance as to how to live a proper human life. That non-Jews have never seen Jews this way is a tragedy of history, but it does not diminish the underlying assumption of how God still hopes the world will work.

---

41. Not all scholars gave blanket permission. Radvaz (R. David ibn Avi Zimra, 1479–1573, Spain, Israel, and Egypt), glossing *Hilchot Melachim* 10:10, forbade non-Jews' fulfilling commandments requiring holiness and purity, such as wearing *tefillin*; R. Moshe Feinstein (1895–1986), *Iggerot Moshe* 2:7, assumed non-Jews could only keep general commandments such as donating to the Temple and giving charity, but none particular to Jews. On the other hand, *Magen Avraham* 304:12 and R. Israel Meir Kagan (1839–1933), *Beur Halachah ad loc,* assumed that a non-Jew could accept certain additional commandments while becoming a resident alien, and those would become permanently obligatory for that non-Jew.
42. *Hilchot Milah* 3:7 and *Responsa* 148.
43. See *Bereshit* 17, *Shabbat* 132a, and *Nedarim* 31b.
44. Rambam's comment, *Guide* III:49, that circumcision serves to reduce sexual desire, and his claim that the foreskin is disgusting, *Hilchot Milah* 3:8, might explain why he allows this for non-Jews as well, since it contributes to the ideal of reining in sexual desire. In his view, it would seem that God made this a sign of the covenant to indicate that sexual restraint is central to Jewish identity.

Conclusion — When Autonomy Yielded to Heteronomy

The model of the world I have tried to elucidate from the Noahide laws differs markedly from that of other religions and from most contemporary writers' views of Judaism. I hope I have shown that Judaism did not see itself as the sole or best way to act *ab initio*, from the beginning of humanity; it assumed people were originally empowered to define their relationship with God almost completely on their own.

Only in response to their crashing failure to do so did God set rules to guide them. While strict, those rules left the basic structure of life — what kind of a job to have, where to focus one's energies in improving the world, how to raise a family, how to use leisure time — to the individual.

That view of the puzzle suggests that Judaism took the Scriptural characterization of its nation as "a kingdom of priests"[45] more literally than sometimes realized. Jewish priests lived markedly different lives from ordinary Jews; their relationship to the Land differed, they were more restricted in whom they could marry or touch, and needed to hold themselves always ready to serve in the Temple if called. This was not a more ideal life, it was a different one, serving one of many important social roles.

The Noahide laws and the sources adduced here show the Talmud viewed Jews as filling a similar role in world society. Like priests, Jews live an unusual life, more narrowly focused on God and ritualistic acts of worship than perhaps necessary for ordinary human beings, in a place with a special connection to God, and were meant to be living representatives of the God Who all humanity are ideally supposed to recognize. The hope was that non-Jews would accept that reality, learn from Jews how to channel their energies — with enormous leeway for how to do so — and live productive lives.

That cannot prove my point about how Jews construct their

---

45. *Shemot* 19:6.

relationship with God, because Jews' more extensive set of laws might have obviated the need for personal input into the relationship with God. The first step on the road to seeing why I disagree with that view is analyzing a crucial episode in the life of the first Jew, the man who straddled the gap between non-Jew and Jew, the Patriarch Avraham.

Chapter 15

Prayer; Avraham's Contribution to Religious Autonomy

For me, Avraham's arguing with God to spare Sodom is another example of the need to restore the crown, where many, perhaps most, readers — with all sincerity — have missed essential parts of the story because of three preconceptions.

First, many people and even some traditional sources assume that prayer is natural, that people always knew they had the right to pray, to ask God to act in a way other than originally planned. Second, a cursory reading of the Biblical text allows the impression that Avraham came up with the idea of praying for Sodom himself. Third, contemporary morality, buttressed by the simplest reading of Avraham's words, would object to God's intention to destroy Sodom because of its inflicting collective punishment, including the righteous with the wicked.

By questioning each of those assumptions, I hope to convince you that the Torah does not show people thinking they could change God's "mind," as it were, before this incident; that it was God Who taught Avraham this human right; and that God also showed Avraham the most effective ways to make such requests. I bring it up here because I believe the kind of petitionary prayer God teaches Avraham once again shows the interplay between heteronomy and autonomy, between slavish obedience and creative response, that I have been laying out.

To begin, I note that we often think of prayer as natural, much as a child calls out to a parent when in trouble. The analogy breaks down when we consider God's omniscience. If God has "chosen" what is happening right now, what could we say that God had not already "thought" of?

Timing the Advent of Petitionary Prayer to Sodom

However we might answer that theoretical problem — and this is not the place for a full or even partial discussion — the Torah itself gives reason to believe Avraham's prayer at Sodom differed qualitatively from earlier ones. To see this, notice that the early chapters of *Bereshit* contain few direct and clearly stated petitionary prayers, if any.

While some texts *can* be read as including a petition — Ramban saw Cain as asking God for a lighter punishment after killing his brother; the Midrash thought Noah prayed for deliverance from the Ark; Rashi thought Avraham asked for a sign to prove that God would fulfill one of his promises; and Ramban thought Avraham meant to ask for Ishmael's life — in none of those cases was the human being seeking a radically different future than the one God intended.[1]

The pre-Sodom sacrifices the Torah records were brought either to thank God or to announce His rule of the world (to be קורא בשם ה', "to call out in the Name of God," in the Biblical phrase), not to petition Him to change the course of history.[2] Yet at Sodom, Avraham stands in God's way, argues the plan should change, and does it remarkably forcefully.

Further indirect support for my claim comes from the two famine stories that sandwich the incident at Sodom. In each of the episodes, Avraham asks Sarah to pose as his sister, fearing the

---

1. Cain says "My sin is too great to bear," *Bereshit* 4:13, which Ramban saw as a prayer for protection from those who would kill him. Aside from the indirect phrasing, it would mean Cain was looking to uphold God's decree, not change it. So, too, Rashi reads Avraham's (*Bereshit* 15:8) "With what shall I know that I will inherit it?" as asking for proof of the promise, not a change of the future. Finally, Ramban reads Avraham's words "Would that Ishmael live before You" (*Bereshit* 17:18) as a prayer that the boy not be killed. While here Ramban may have assumed Avraham was trying to change the planned future, the request is indirect, almost as if expressing a wish in God's hearing was the most he was allowed to do.
2. See, for example, *Bereshit* 10:8.

people would kill him to get to her. In the first instance, Pharaoh's officers praise her to the king and she is taken to his palace, apparently to become his wife or concubine. God afflicts the Egyptians in response, which Pharaoh relates to Sarah's arrival. Chastened, he returns Sarah with many gifts, and they leave the area.

In chapter 20, the first story after the Torah finishes with Sodom and its aftermath, Avraham goes to Gerar. Events proceed similarly to Egypt, except that when the king of Gerar takes Sarah, God appears to Avimelech in a dream to warn him of his impending doom. Avimelech protests his innocence, correctly noting he did not know Sarah was Avraham's wife. God agrees, yet still orders him to ask Avraham to pray for him — the first appearance of the verb root פלל ("to pray") in Scripture.

The Torah does not explain the paradox of God's accepting Avimelech's claims of innocence while still requiring him to ask Avraham to pray. Seeing Sodom as when Avraham himself learned about prayer explains the matter. In Egypt, prayer could not be a factor, since Avraham did not yet know of his right to pray. At that point, Avraham was wandering the world, dependent on God's protection, becoming wealthy and famous.

When he moved to Gerar, though, he had new knowledge to share with others. To insure Avimelech would learn that lesson, God insisted he ask Avraham to pray.[3] Rather than simply repeating an earlier incident, the second famine story shows Avraham's growth, and the broader set of ideas about God he was now able to teach.

---

3. R. Achituv, *Megadim* (No. 31, Tevet 5760, Winter 2000), "שומע תפילה במקרא, The One Who Hears Prayers in Scripture," notes that prayer in Scripture is generally offered by prophets or functionaries of the Temple. On 109, he refers to the incident with Avimelech as proof of his contention — Avimelech's prayers are unacceptable, but Avraham's will be accepted. He does not explain why Avimelech had to pray at all, since he had done no wrong, leading me to prefer my reading.

Time and Place: Sodom as the Paradigm for Prayer in Avraham's Life

The possibility that Avraham first learned about prayer at Sodom enriches the Talmudic reading of Avraham's actions the morning after. The Torah reports that the next morning, Avraham rose early ("וישכם") "to the place where he had stood there before God,"[4] which the Talmud interprets as a veiled reference to prayer, fueling its belief that Avraham instituted שחרית, the Morning Prayer.[5]

The Talmud does not say that Avraham decided to institute daily morning prayer *because* of the incident with Sodom, but the verse is suggestive. Just after a discussion with God where prayer was a central issue, the Torah uses a verb that to the Talmud means Avraham instituted regular morning prayer. So, too, this reading illuminates the Talmud's claim that Avraham also went to the same *place* as where he had prayed for Sodom, fueling its preference that we all should pray at a fixed personal venue.[6]

If prayer was always part of Avraham's life, there would be no reason for this place and time of day to attain such significance. If, on the other hand, this was where he first learned his right to pray, we can well understand why he would be so moved that he would use it to anchor all his future prayer experiences.

God's Invitation

The Scriptural recounting of the event itself provides more evidence for my claim. The Torah records God's words prior to His discussion with Avraham. Explaining His decision to tell Avraham about Sodom ahead of time, the Torah quotes God as saying:

> Shall I hide from Avraham that which I intend to do... for
> I have known him in order that (Heb.: למען) he command

---

4. *Bereshit* 19:27.
5. *Ber.* 26b.
6. *Ber.* 6b.

his sons and household after him that they shall guard
the path of God, to perform justice and righteousness.[7]

The first key to understanding the passage is remembering that
when Scripture reports God's thoughts, it is using a literary device
to inform us of underlying aspects of the action we would not
otherwise understand. God does not "think," at least not in the
way we do, and God does not justify to Himself, as it were, the
decisions He makes. These verses, properly read, are there to tell
us something, to set up a framework we might not have known
from the rest of the text.

To understand that framework, we have to realize how incom-
plete God's words are. God seems to say He cannot hide what He
wants to do from Avraham, because He has known Avraham so
that he will teach his descendants about justice and righteousness,
but we are not told the connection between telling Avraham about
Sodom and God's having known him, nor how that knowledge
would facilitate Avraham's teaching his descendants about God.

The question has been answered numerous times,[8] none
of which I find fully satisfactory, but I think Ramban offers a

---

7. *Bereshit* 18:19.
8. Rashi thinks God was saying that since Avraham will command his
   descendants to follow God's path, God "has" to tell Avraham about
   Sodom's impending doom. That reading interprets the two appearances
   of the word למען differently in the same sentence — once as "because"
   and once as "in order that." Also, that does not explain why the Torah
   told us of each of Avraham's arguments on Sodom's behalf.

   Others, such as the late fifteenth-century Don Isaac Abarbanel and
   the early sixteenth-century Italian Jewish commentator Sforno, saw
   God as telling Avraham about Sodom to reassure him of the justice of
   their destruction. The details of Avraham's protests, in this view, show
   us that he fully explored the issue by exhausting all possible options. He
   could then walk away renewed in his dedication to raise children who
   would follow the paths of the Lord.

   Their reading, to my mind, makes the questionable assumption that
   without the prior conversation, Avraham would have had doubts about
   God's justice, a view that stands at odds with Avraham's later willingness
   to kill Yitschak unquestioningly.

promising start. Ramban reads "כי ידעתיו למען" ("for I have known him so that") as meaning that God has cultivated His relationship with Avraham to prepare the Patriarch to properly teach his descendants how to serve Him. In this view, God's "knowing" of Avraham is the only way Avraham would have been able to raise a family properly dedicated to God's service.

That already contributes to our broader discussion, reminding us that at least some of God's commandments are there to foster our understanding of how to worship God properly. Since God extends that idea to telling Avraham about Sodom, Ramban would seem to be implying that here, too, God is easing Avraham's ability to prepare his descendants for a life of service to God.

Reading that interpretation back into God's words produces the following translation: "Will I hide from Avraham what I am going to do to Sodom [thus missing an opportunity to educate him about how to serve Me], when Avraham is going to be a great and mighty nation, in whom all the nations of the world will be blessed? For [after all] I have known Avraham [gotten him to the point that he would be the progenitor of this great nation] so that he can command his descendants after him, etc."[9]

The Lesson of Prayer

God's words tell us that He sees the coming conversation as part of the education of a Patriarch, but the conversation itself gives us the content of that lesson. God tells Avraham He *intends* to descend to the city of Sodom, to *check* whether the reports about it are true, in which case He will destroy the city.[10]

---

9. The nineteenth-century R. Naftali Zvi Yehuda Berlin (Netsiv) saw this incident as educating Avraham about how God deals with evildoers, which at least agrees that the conversation sought to educate Avraham. Rambam includes the verse למען אשר יצוה ("in order that he should command") twice in the tenth chapter of his *Hilchot Matnot Aniyim*, in paragraphs one and fifteen, in the specific context of prayer; although he does not explain, his citation suggests a similar sense of the text.

10. *Bereshit* 18:21. For comparison, note that in *Shemot* 3:9 and I *Shmuel*

Since Avraham knew as well as we do that God does not need to investigate a situation in order to ascertain the facts, His phrasing it that way seems to call for a human response,[11] as if God were opening the floor to discussion and debate. Despite an existing plan for how the future would unfold — the cities would be wiped out, righteous with the wicked — the right arguments could perhaps affect it.

The Torah then tells us all the details of the ensuing discussion, itself surprising. If the central point of telling us about Avraham's prayer was to show his concern for Sodom, it seems odd that the Torah would tell us each detail of his failed attempt, noble as it might be — let the Torah tell us Avraham prayed, and leave it at that. It makes more sense, I propose, that we are supposed to note the act itself, with each detail adding to our understanding.[12]

In other words, I am suggesting that the very shape of the conversation suggests that God was showing Avraham his *right* to pray, tolerantly replying to each of his attempts, simply to encourage the endeavor itself. By doing so here, God was encouraging prayer even when seemingly hopeless; since people cannot distinguish final from conditional decrees, they can and should always try praying for a different outcome.

Arguing For Sodom — A Manual of Prayer

But a closer look shows God went further; by informing Avraham that He was going to see whether "as their cries, they had done," God invited the Patriarch to offer a different view the situation. After all, nothing God would find upon going to see would change

---

9:16, God also mentions that cries have reached Him. In each of those cases, God is taking action in response, not "going down" to check the accuracy of those cries.

11. The way God opens a conversation with humans is often instructive, as Rashi noted on God's words to Moshe at the Golden Calf (*Shemot* 32:10), to Adam (*Bereshit* 3:9), and to Balaam (*Bamidbar* 22:9).

12. My thanks to R. Barry Kornblau for questioning why God would encourage Avraham to pray in a futile situation.

the facts, so there would seem little for Avraham to contribute. The open question was whether Avraham could successfully militate for a different reaction to those facts.

Which is what Avraham does, although we only realize that when we read his words carefully. The simplest reading leads to the widespread view that he was decrying the apparent injustice of God's plan to kill the righteous with the wicked — "Will you destroy the righteous with the wicked…it is profane for you to kill the righteous with the wicked…shall the Judge of the entire earth not execute justice?"[13]

I cannot accept that reading, though, for the significant philosophical and textual problems it raises. First, it makes the premise of the conversation untenable in one of two ways. If Avraham is protesting the morality of God's intention to kill the few righteous with the many wicked — and we accept both that God *had* intended to do that *and* that it is immoral — we would have Scriptural evidence of a human being giving a basic morality lesson to the Creator; I reject that categorically.

Slightly less problematic is to assume that God did *not* intend to kill the righteous, and Avraham's whole complaint was based on a mistaken assumption. But then why would God let Avraham go on at such length, agonizing over a course of action God had never contemplated *and* record it in full in the Torah? It would have been simpler for God to interrupt the first time, say, "Listen, Avraham, there aren't any righteous people in Sodom, and if there are, I will not kill them with the wicked."

A Missed Implication of Avraham's Prayer

Another problem with the common reading of Avraham's opening complaint becomes clear when we add back a piece of the text I omitted above. In addition to his other claims, Avraham also says, "Will You destroy and not bear the place for the sake of the fifty righteous in its midst?" Avraham was not arguing to

---

13. *Bereshit* 18:23–25.

save Sodom's *righteous*, he was going a step further, claiming their presence should forestall the destruction of the *evildoers* as well.

If so, we can no longer take his protest of killing the righteous with the wicked in its simplest sense, since if that was the only problem, God could have extracted them, as He does with Lot. Why would Avraham jump to ask God to save the wicked?

What seems more likely is that Avraham and God both knew the question at hand was the fate of the cities *as a whole*. Modern morality dismisses corporate responsibility or collective judgment, but I am not convinced that Judaism does (see, for example, the laws of an עיר הנדחת, a city where the majority of its citizens have worshipped idolatry, or the rules for cities the Jews conquered).

Once we understand that Sodom and the other cities were to live or die as a unit, Avraham's words become instantly more comprehensible. Rather than objecting to the idea of killing the righteous with the wicked *per se*, he was protesting that the presence of the righteous might give reason to stay God's hand on the *whole* city, presumably because those righteous might still have a positive impact on the larger entity. Treating a group as a unit means judging them as a whole, but Avraham argues that it should also extend to assessing their likelihood of improvement as a unit.

The decision to destroy Sodom focused on the sinners, whose acts and overwhelming influence on society more than justified the annihilation of the city, including any relative innocents. Avraham raised the possibility that even just fifty righteous people might change that, making it unjust to take away that chance.

Given a little time, I read Avraham as arguing, the Fifty could change the cities so that they would no longer deserve annihilation, an outcome that better reflects the balance between justice and mercy portrayed elsewhere in Scripture. Avraham's plea was not a protest of God's injustice so much as a hope that God would make room for a less likely option whose incalculably better upsides made it worth the risk of failure.

"Will You destroy the righteous with the wicked?" is not

aimed at saving the righteous, it is asking for more time for them to positively influence the wicked. It is better read, then, as "Will You destroy righteous and wicked together? Perhaps there are fifty righteous people [who can affect the character of the city]; will you erase and not give the place [more time] for the sake of the fifty?" So, too, "shall the Judge of the Earth not do justice" refers to the justice of giving sinners every possible opportunity, however slim, to find a way to step back from their evil and repent of their sins.[14]

"Convinced," God accedes to his prayers.

This reading of the story also translates into a productive new paradigm for successful petitionary prayer. While the supplicant must always submit to God's view of the world and how it should work, prayer is an opportunity to suggest other ways of achieving God's goals. The petitioner stands at the edge of a worrisome future; often, that person will just beg God for another chance, for a better outcome. Avraham suggests that a better strategy is to articulate how a hoped-for alternative will lead to a better fulfillment of God's wishes for the world.

I see this ability to argue in favor of a less likely path, to commit to working to bring that path into reality, as the gift God gave Avraham at Sodom. Looking at how it plays out in the rest of Scripture, we will see more clearly how it can affect our prayers and our understanding of the kind of balance between obedience and independence God seeks from us.

---

14. This also explains Avraham's dogged pursuit of ever lower numbers. The bigger the core of righteous people, the greater their chance of success. Rashi assumed the righteous might be spread among the five cities, giving further reason to test each new number of righteous. If five cities each contain a coterie of righteous people (a Morality Institute, perhaps with panel discussions and public lectures), they would wield greater influence than if any of them stood as lone voices in a sea of wickedness. Each reduction in the number of cities containing such people would raise new doubts about the odds of their meaningfully affecting their own city, and also whether their presence should affect God's decision.

Chapter 16

The Lessons of Prayer

There are several examples of prayer after Avraham, but the first that most clearly echoes the ideas we saw in the previous chapter is that of Moshe Rabbenu after the sin of the Golden Calf. The conversation between God and Moshe at that incident shows that, despite Moshe having prayed many times before, God taught him a significant lesson about prayer at this crucial juncture.

The way the Torah speaks of Moshe's early petitions suggests it was not a natural skill. When Pharaoh asks Moshe to pray to end a plague, Scripture uses the verb העתרה ("to entreat").[1] The Torah describes Moshe as צועק ("shouts out"),[2] פורש כפים ("spreads his hands"),[3] and מעתיר, all verbs of notable effort.[4] The master of prophets, at this stage, seems unsure of how to speak effectively to the living God.

His early difficulties contrast remarkably with his handling of two later incidents. When God afflicts Miriam with leprosy, Moshe successfully elicits relief in just five words.[5] A chapter later, when God mentions destroying the Jewish people, Moshe composes a lengthy, eloquent prayer that elicits the desired response:

---

1. *Shemot* 8:4 and 24, and 9:28.
2. Ibid., 8:8.
3. Ibid., 8:29. I construe Moshe's extending his hands in prayer as an intensification of the experience.
4. Ibid., 9:29.
5. Admittedly, for this prayer he was צועק, "cried out." Perhaps the difficulty stems from the prayer's brevity, lack of argumentation, and hurried composition, not a discomfort with formulating effective prayer.

"סלחתי כדבריך, I have forgiven as per your request."[6] Elsewhere, the text uses the simple verb ויתפלל, and he prayed.[7]

Looking now at the interaction after the sin of the Golden Calf, we can see how God trained Moshe how to pray, feeding him the arguments that would allow him to avert the people's destruction. The Torah records the Jews' sin in chapter 32 of *Shemot*, followed in verses 7–14 by God and Moshe's dialogue. The relevant text reads:

> God spoke to Moshe: "Go, descend — for your people that you brought up from the land of Egypt has become corrupt. [8]They have strayed quickly from the way that I have commanded them. They have made themselves a molten calf, prostrated themselves to it and sacrificed to it, and they said: 'This is your god, O Israel, which brought you up from the land of Egypt.'" [9]God said to Moshe, "I have seen this people, and behold! It is a stiff-necked people; [10]And now, desist from Me. Let My anger flare up against them, and I shall annihilate them; and I shall make you a great nation." [11]Moshe supplicated before God, his Lord, and said: "Why, God, should Your anger flare up against Your people, whom You have taken out of the land of Egypt, with great power and with a strong hand? [12]Why should Egypt say the following: 'With evil intent did He take them out, to kill them in the mountains and to annihilate them from the face of the earth? Relent from Your flaring anger and reconsider regarding the evil against Your people. [13]Remember for the sake of Avraham, Isaac, and Israel, Your servants, to whom You swore by Yourself, and You told them, 'I shall increase your offspring like the stars of heaven, and this

---

6. *Bamidbar* 14:18.
7. *Bamidbar* 11:2, 21:7, and *Devarim* 9:20, where Moshe terms his prayers for Aaron after the Golden Calf a תפילה.

entire land of which I spoke, I shall give to your offspring
and it will be their heritage forever.

A thousand years ago, Rashi already understood that God's telling
Moshe to "desist from Me" really said the opposite, told him he
had the right to keep pleading.[8] Taking that insight further, I note
that every one of God's utterances frames Moshe's reply. God tells
Moshe that *his* (Moshe's) people, the ones *he* (Moshe) took out
of Egypt, have sinned, quickly leaving the path of righteousness,
making other gods, and declaring them their own; now, God says,
leave Me alone and I will allow My anger to destroy them.

God's words deny all connection with the people — they are
Moshe's, not His. This severing "allows" God to react with the
full harshness appropriate to their act. Partners to a long-term
bond bear an obligation to view any act, no matter how egregious,
through the prism of the entire relationship, which might reduce
the impact of this one incident; a slap in the face administered
by a stranger is different from the same physical act coming
from a close friend or relative. Denying that connection, then, is
a first step to justifying the Jews' destruction, which which they
deserved at the time.

Themes of Effective Prayer

Moshe takes up each claim in turn. First, they are not his people
but God's, whom God took out of Egypt. Further, not only are
they God's people, God deliberately publicized their leaving
Egypt to convey His power not just to the Jews, but the world at
large. Should God now destroy the people, He would completely
negate the lesson — a lesson the Jews themselves have learned
insufficiently, as their sin shows. Finally, while God asks Moshe
for permission, as it were, to destroy the Jews, Moshe notes that
he, Moshe, cannot grant it, since God must fulfill the promises
to the Patriarchs.

---

8. Verse 10, commenting on the words הניחה לי, desist from Me.

As with Avraham, God's omniscience should mean He knew Moshe's arguments even before they were said; that God raised each of the points Moshe used in response suggests the introduction was a guide. Indeed, Moshe's themes in his plea remain those in use until this day: showing how it would be inappropriate or ineffective (in God's terms) to continue as we fear the Divine Plan dictates.

The Jews who left Egypt were the fulfillment of God's promise to the Patriarchs and the living embodiment of God's singular power, His ability to reduce even the strongest nation in the world to abject submission. Moshe seems to be "reminding" God of His relationship with the Patriarchs, who taught the world of His existence, and the Jews whom He took out of Egypt, who served as His representatives to the world.

Moshe's experience confirms the lessons of Avraham's prayer at Sodom, that petitionary prayer ideally combines absorbing God's plans and goals for the world — a heteronomous experience — with the autonomous human ability to formulate plausible alternate ways of reaching those goals.

Hannah's Contribution to Prayer

Hannah's prayer for a son highlights that mode of autonomous petition. Although Hannah had many personal reasons to want a son, Scripture only mentions the vow she took, to dedicate the child to God, to make him a Nazirite all his days.[9] That is a promise, not a prayer; Scripture's characterizing it as one makes sense if her promise was the kind of reasoning that would make prayers successful, a way to show that her personal desires would actually further God's goals for the world.[10] God's plan did not include a child for Hannah (for reasons of His inscrutable Will);

9. I *Shmuel* 1:11.
10. See I *Shmuel* 1:10–12. The text says that Hannah prayed, and then records her vow. Even if we assume that she prayed in addition to the vow, the text still characterizes the vow as part of her prayer.

her unusual willingness to dedicate the child completely to the Lord presented a less obvious plan, but one that furthered God's goals even better, giving God a prophet to spread His words and service among the people.

Thus, while prayer expresses human autonomy to reimagine the future, it only became available by God's having shown it to us on several different crucial occasions. Further, it seems to work best when humans find alternative ways of achieving *God's* goals; the successful supplicant will have to immerse him- or herself in God's worldview before he or she could possibly understand a future to suggest. Consistent with my general theme, we find broad autonomy that results from a dose of heteronomy.

Voluntary Modes of Worship: The Lost World of Avraham

Avraham is sometimes seen as the paradigmatic Noahide, since the Talmud assumes that Biblical statements about Avraham inform us as to the extent of Noahide obligations.[11] He is also העברי, the one on the other side, separate and distinct from the rest of the world. Similarly, while he obviously observed all the Noahide laws, much of what he became famous for — welcoming guests, building altars to call out in the Name of God, trying to convince others of the truth of monotheism — was not in the Noahide code, was Avraham's understanding of how a God-focused individual should act.

Returning to prayer, we can now appreciate that it is but one example of a broader aspect of Avraham's life. God taught Avraham he was allowed to pray, but Avraham decided to institute regular morning prayer. Tradition sees the next two Patriarchs as each instituting one further prayer, suggesting they had learned from their father the importance of innovating in one's worship of God.

Indeed, Rambam thinks Avraham articulated an entire

---

11. *Sanhedrin* 56b.

tradition of how to live a God-centered life.[12] In his view, the Jews' descent to Egypt and the influence of idol worship destroyed the Patriarchs' legacy, making clear that a voluntary system would not work. Moshe's contribution, for Rambam, was to convey God's decision to legislate, with reward and punishment ensuring that the system — probably similar to the one Avraham enunciated — would take hold and last.[13]

How Important Is The Commanded Aspect of *Mitzvot*?

Rambam's idea of a voluntary religion formulated by human beings, even Avraham, runs counter to the stress on *mitzvot* many assume is so central to Judaism. We will get to *mitzvot*, but already here Rambam's picture encourages us to question whether commandments were always part of the Divine plan. In his view, it seems, had Avraham's descendants and students maintained their commitment to his principles and practices, the events at Sinai might have been unnecessary, or at least radically different.

That would seem to reject the literal meaning of the Talmudic claim that the Patriarch kept the entire Torah, and call into question the ordinary reading of several other Talmudic statements as well. Focusing on a few will prepare us for the next chapter, where

---

12. See his presentation at the beginning of *Hilchot Avodah Zarah*. While many assume the Talmud meant *Yoma* 28b's claim that Avraham kept the entire Torah literally, Rambam probably understood it to mean that he observed all the underlying principles and purposes of the system commanded at Sinai.

13. In addition to ibid., see his presentation of the evolution of commandments in *Hilchot Melachim* 9:1. Note that Rambam sees Avraham, Yitschak, and Yaacov as undertaking various acts on their own, but Amram, in Egypt, as commanded. See also *Guide* II:13, where the belief that God created the world is repeatedly credited to both Avraham and Moshe. I first heard this reconstruction of Rambam's ideas from Aviezer Ravitsky at Harvard University in Spring 1993; it is now, I believe, commonplace.

we show that *mitzvot* themselves were not meant as the sum total of how one worshipped God.

Berachot 8b says that from the day the Temple was destroyed, all God has in this world are the four cubits of *halachah*. On its face, the statement suggests that God's concerns narrowed with the destruction, that all He currently "cares" about is *halachah* and its observance. One problem with that is that the Temple was not the only focus of God's concern in the world when it was standing, so there is no reason its destruction would restrict God's concerns so radically.

It seems more likely that the Talmud is arguing that the world of *halachah* substituted for one or most functions of the Temple, much as prayer came to substitute for the sacrifices. The easiest possibility would be that *halachah* took over the Temple's role as a location where people could directly experience God.[14] The Destruction took away the Temple's ability to serve in that particular area of religious experience, and *halachah* took it over. In terms of direct connection with people, God only has *halachah* now. But it does not mean, either during the time of the Temple or after, that that is all that matters in God's universe.

The Talmud's rule that גדול המצווה ועושה משאינו מצווה ועושה, one who is commanded to perform an act is greater than one who performs the same act without being commanded,[15] is also often taken as demonstrating a general preference for heteronomy over autonomy. Here too, a moment's reflection reminds us that the statement compares performances of a *particular* act; it does not mean that an obligated person who recites Grace After Meals, for example, is necessarily greater than one who voluntarily studies the entirety of Torah or visits the sick. The Talmud only means that *once* God obligated certain people in certain ways, they receive the greatest reward for fulfilling those obligations.[16]

---

14. R. Soloveitchik is reported to have noted that Scripture describes the experience of being at the Temple as being לפני ה', before God.

15. *Kiddushin* 31a.

16. Incidentally, the expectation of reward for voluntary performance is

Although the Giving of the Law at Sinai is the central event of the Jewish religion, our thrust so far has been to show that there is room within Jewish sources to recognize that its legislative content might have been shaped differently had human history progressed along other lines. Had Noahides recognized their responsibility to serve God in all the ways a reasonably intuitive person would, or had Avraham's students and descendants done a better job of handling his legacy, the Revelation at Sinai might have been of a different sort altogether, and we might today adhere to a system largely defined by humans. Working with Divine guidance, of course, but with rules and details of our own making.

That realization has absolutely no practical ramifications, since we cannot turn back time. Seeing what might have been serves a positive function, however, in preparing us to look with new eyes at the system that developed, letting us see that much as the system was and is concerned with punctilious observance of specific rituals, it was and is even more interested in those observances serving as a launching pad for each individual's discovery of his or her own best ways to serve God.

---

not as obvious as we take it. It is at least possible that acts obligatory upon one set of people are not particularly desirable for another set. The Talmud might have meant, then, that the *metsuveh ve-oseh* is greater because only he can be sure his act is wholly positive. Along these lines, see *Derashot haRan*, Sermon 13, who argues that God's commandments are so specifically tailored that only those commanded to perform an act can fully accomplish its goals.

Chapter 17

Mitzvot and their Blank Spaces

O f all the areas of human activity, *mitzvot* would seem least amenable to personal choices, since they are, by definition, commandments. There is some human input in understanding the Biblical and Talmudic texts that define those *mitzvot,* since traditional sources recognize that the Biblical text leaves room for differences of interpretation that produce *halachically* different outcomes. For an easy example, *halachah* recognizes that in different generations courts might apply the rules of interpretation to the same Biblical text and come to differing conclusions about what the Torah wants from us.[1]

That form of autonomy is too limited to interest me here, since all such readings are an attempt to recover the original intent of the text, in all its legal, spiritual, and conceptual ramifications. While it may be a part of the human condition that we differ even in our best efforts in this regard, the only hoped-for originality in this context is in achieving truer insight into what God and the Torah wanted. This is not autonomy; it is a recognition of the necessary barriers we strive to overcome in searching for an externally determined truth.[2]

---

1. *Hilchot Mamrim* 1:2, but I don't think the point is disputed.
2. R. Soloveitchik's philosophical writings stressed exactly this kind of autonomy. For him, Torah scholars' innovative understandings of tradition revolutionarily impacted the world of Torah and *mitzvot*. I am arguing here that the system also sought a much broader autonomy from all people, one that moved beyond (without in any way discarding) the *mitzvot*.

Central *Mitzvot* as Exemplars of the Need for Personal Input

It is much better for my argument that numerous central requirements of the religion are expressed so loosely as to necessitate significant personal decisions about how to achieve the Torah's desideratum. Filling in these blanks is a personal matter, although *Hazal* and later Jewish literature often provide guidance. By looking at some of the most basic of those obligations, I hope to show how the very fabric of a Jew's life is or ought to be set by each Jew for him- or herself, albeit with an eye towards whatever guidance Torah teachers and texts can provide. This is even more true for non-Jews, whose laws are so much more minimal.

Proving this contention for all the *mitzvot* requires a book of its own, so I will take seven commandments as a representative sample — to love God, follow His ways, study Torah, rest on Shabbat, rest on the various holidays, give charity, and honor one's parents. I hope that as we go along, you will see that the seven show a system where commandments are the necessary basis of our actions, but only the basis, not the sum total of the expected actions.

I chose these seven because they highlight the extent to which the system forces people to make significant religious choices. Try as we might to hide in the world of law, these *mitzvot* — some of the most central to being a Jew, theologically and experientially — show that a true religious life involves decisions that are not and cannot be subordinated to the commands of tradition.[3]

Love of God

The centrality of the *mitzvah* to love God, if not inherently obvious, expresses itself first in the fact that it is one of the six that

---

3. Note that I am not implying that Jews were supposed to come up with *new* laws, a clear prohibition. It is in applying minimally defined *mitzvot* that Judaism leaves Jews maximum room to integrate the religion's stated concerns with his or her own interests and talents.

obligates all Jews at all times and places. In addition, men at least had to recite the words "ואהבת את ה' אלוקיך, you shall love the Lord your God" twice a day.[4] As I noted in the first part of this book, that which we are told to speak about more consistently and frequently is more central to our lived lives.

Defining that obligation presents significant challenges. The Torah seems to be commanding an emotion, difficult when it comes to a Supreme Being. Love ordinarily involves a sense of deep identification, a connection based on blood relationship, living together, or shared interests. God's Otherness would seem to preclude that form of love, leaving unclear what the Torah seeks in this commandment.

Rashi and Ramban offer one way around the problem. They assume that ואהבת, love, refers to performing *mitzvot* מאהבה, out of love, which they define as without any ulterior motive. This view relates love to לשמה, performing these acts simply because God commanded them, without any interest in rewards that accrue from such performance.[5] The love of *ve-ahavta*, for these commentators, is at least partially expressed in the underlying motivation in submitting to God's rule.[6]

The Emotion of Love of God in Rambam's View

Rambam takes the requirement of love more literally. Early in the

---

4. *Devarim* 6:5.
5. Judaism's defining love as fulfilling *mitzvot* out of pure obedience seems to run counter to my endeavor here, as well as to the project of ta`amei hamitzvot, finding reasons and rationales for the commandments. The contradiction falls away when we recognize that the rock-bottom motivation that insures observance can differ from the experience of *mitzvot*; we ultimately keep the commandments because God told us to do so, but our experience of those *mitzvot* can, should, and must be informed and enriched by understanding the contribution this particular observance makes to the entire framework of Torah.
6. I see no reason Rashi and Ramban could not accept Rambam's view of love of God as well.

first book of the *Mishneh Torah*, *Laws of the Foundations of the Torah*, he notes that contemplating the wonders of the created universe engenders a sense of love for the One who put all this into place.[7] The love that comes from this experience, it seems, parallels the human love that arises in gratitude for a longstanding relationship of giving. That might only be a starting point, but for Rambam, a Jew builds love for the Creator by contemplating His kindnesses and the wondrous world He created.

Later in that section, Rambam records the Talmudic claim that foregoing certain kinds of medical treatment constitutes a fulfillment of the obligation to love God even at the cost of one's life.[8] He closes the section by writing of constant, almost obsessive, focus on God as either itself constituting love or helping to build it.[9] Although commonly thought of as an arch-rationalist, Rambam tells us the relationship he is describing is parallel to that of a lovesick man who thinks about his beloved constantly.

He does not mean the person simply states his or her love of God, just as human love does not consist solely of what one says. Rather, the person is always thinking of God, just as one in love cannot get his or her mind off of the beloved. The basic principle seems to be that *acting* as if one is in love, using the human tools of constancy of concern and thought, will lead towards love itself.

Particularly since he explicitly relates love of God to human love, Rambam seems clear about the personal aspect of this *mitzvah*, at least in the first and third examples he gave. Humans differ in how they appreciate Creation, which would imply that we will contemplate God's role in that creation from different perspectives and with varying emphases. We each have our individual approaches in our expressions of our human love and so with the Creator. As such, the commandment shifts with each Jew, meaning, at least in Rambam's presentation, that each Jew must

---

7. *Hilchot Yesodei haTorah* 2:2. The experience also fuels *yir'ah*, awe.
8. Ibid., 5:7.
9. *Hilchot Teshuvah* 10:3 and 6.

construct a personal and loving relationship with God, going beyond the programmed, as in his or her other relationships.

To Mold One's Character to Become "Similar" to Him

The Torah repeatedly refers to the requirement to follow His ways, ללכת בדרכיו,[10] which we might have taken as referring to *mitzvot*, the "ways" God commanded. Rambam, based on several rabbinic statements (and without serious dispute from others), understands this *mitzvah* to include personal character development. For him, that meant the Aristotelian middle path.

Judging one's character traits and how best to bring them more to the perfect middle is, however, an inherently individualized activity; the person can seek advice from a sage or counselor, but the actual efforts will need to be defined and executed by that person alone.

Rambam expands our understanding of his idea by his differing presentations in his various works. In *Sefer haMitzvot*, he cites the Midrash[11] rather than the Talmud. Commenting on the words ללכת בכל דרכיו, to walk in all His ways,[12] the Midrash says, "Just as He is called חנון (compassionate), so you be *hanun*; just as He is called, etc." The Midrash does not claim God *is* compassionate, merciful, or any of the other listed traits, just that he is *called* such.

Given Rambam's concerns about ascribing emotions and actions to God, the Midrash's saying only that God is *called* those characteristics serves the vital function of maintaining a distinction between God and humans; Scripture uses certain words

---

10. For some examples, see *Devarim* 8:6, 10:12, 11:22, 19:9. Note that in each, the Torah juxtaposes "following His ways" to some other experience, fear, love, or cleaving to Him, as if the "following" leads to or is the result of the others.
11. *Yalkut Shimoni Parshat Ekev*, Paragraph 873.
12. *Devarim* 10:12 and 11:22.

for God not because they are accurate but because they instruct people as to how to best improve *their* character.

Two other of his sources complicate the picture. First, the verse "אחרי ה' אלוקיכם תלכו, You shall follow after the Lord Your God"[13] leads the Talmud to assert that God's clothing the naked (Adam and Eve), visiting the sick (Avraham after his circumcision), and comforting the bereaved (after Sarah died), obligates humans to do so as well.[14] In contrast to the Midrash, the Talmud stressed God's *acting* in those ways, suggesting that the obligation to follow His ways is more literal than Rambam saw it in *Sefer haMitzvot*.

This may not go that much farther than the Midrash, since it only calls on us to imitate God's actions as they impact this world. We might claim that here, too, the Talmud really only meant that God is *described* as acting a certain way, a metaphor for saying we should just learn a lesson from the Torah's description.

Rambam also cites Abba Shaul's statement, recorded in the Talmud, that the verse "זה א-לי ואנוהו, this is my God and I will glorify Him"[15] means that just as God is חנון, so, too, Jews have to be חנון, and so on, leaving out the crucial words "is called."[16] Here, the verse speaks only of identifying and glorifying God, but Abba Shaul reads it as requiring us to become *like* God, apparently assuming those terms describe God.

Rambam's explanation of this last source helps us understand his view of the *mitzvah*. He says that God's impact on this world — not *how* He does it, but the results of His influence — would, if a human were to have such impact, betray certain traits of character, particularly those listed in the 13 Attributes so central to the liturgy of Yom Kippur.[17] Those character traits are binding,

---

13. *Devarim* 14:5.
14. *Sotah* 14a.
15. *Shemot* 15:2.
16. *Guide* I:54. Rambam cites the *Midrash* on *Parshat Kedoshim*; we have it in *Shabbat* 133b.
17. *Shemot* 34:6.

and it is in that sense that we can meaningfully say that God is compassionate (He has created a world which, if a human had created it, would betray its Creator's compassion) or any other such description.

This *mitzvah*, then, calls on human beings' best powers of discernment. While one view of character formation is to adopt the Golden Mean, the descriptions of God in Scripture are at least partially intended as a paradigm of the kinds of acts and emotions to cultivate. Finally, the world also provides evidence of God's character, obligating us to extrapolate from the world to figure out how to mold ourselves in more God-like ways.

Obviously, in a world as multifaceted as ours, there can be almost an infinite number of productive and positive versions of an ideal character. Depending on personal proclivities and with only skeletal *halachic* guidance, Jews seeking to imitate God will necessarily differ in which aspects of the world they emphasize in shaping themselves. Some might focus on how God sustains all living creatures and enter or volunteer for wildlife conservation; others might think of how God feeds the hungry and seek to alleviate the plight of the poor.

Trying to help the poor could itself fuel numerous equally legitimate paths: some might choose to study agriculture or plant biology to make food more readily available in impoverished parts of the world; others might study economics to identify and remedy inequities; others might enter politics to try to implement those ideas; others might actively collect excess food and distribute it to those in need. As with loving God, the *mitzvah* leaves to individual choice much more than I think is often realized.

Talmud Torah — Transmitting Cultural Knowledge

Three points Rambam includes in describing the *mitzvah* of studying Torah show God was interested in more than the act itself. The first two — that the verse says ושננתם לבניך, you shall teach it to your children,[18] and that the *Sifre* rules that this obligates teaching any students who wish to learn, since Scripture elsewhere refers to students as sons[19] — show that the focus is less on study than transmission to sons or students.

Rambam also cites *Sifre's* nonliteral reading of ושננתם, which midrashically twists the word so that it can mean we are obligated to know the literature of Torah well enough to answer all questions immediately. The derivation is only persuasive for those who accept Midrashic hermeneutics (rules for reading texts), but *Sifre* is saying, at least in part, that the point of study and knowledge is so that others have access to it.

Further examples only ratify that the *mitzvah* seeks more than the act of study. Rambam follows the Talmud in assigning grandfathers a greater obligation to teach grandchildren than the ordinary one for Jews to teach others who wish to learn.[20] This grandparental duty — as we noted in the first part of this book, almost unique in Jewish literature[21] — also points to the *mitzvah* as a way to guarantee knowledge-transmission throughout the generations. Fathers are most responsible for that goal, but grandfathers are not far behind.

Remembering Sinai, Focusing on the Written Torah

The verse that led the Talmud to recognize a grandparental role enhances our sense of Torah as being about more than personal study in another way. As we noted in the first part, the Talmud and Rambam read *Devarim* 4:9, ostensibly warning us not to

---

18. *Devarim* 6:7.
19. *Shemot* 34:7.
20. Based on the verse והודעתם לבניך ולבני בניך, you shall make them known to your sons and grandsons. *Devarim* 4:9; see *Hilchot Talmud Torah* 1:2, from *Kiddushin* 30a.
21. *Shemot* 10:2 refers to telling our children and grandchildren of how God toyed with the Egyptians, but that is not in the context of a *mitzvah*, nor is it codified by *halachah*.

forget the Giving of the Law at Sinai, as relating to Torah study in general. Another part of teaching Torah to our descendants is keeping alive memory of the original event.

The definition of the minimum fulfillment of the *mitzvah*, either the Five Books of the Torah or, perhaps, the entirety of Scripture,[22] cuts in the same direction. The definition of "teaching" is not fully clear — it might mean the child knows the Torah well enough to recite it by heart or could read from the Torah in synagogue on command, to pick two maximalist versions of the obligation — but it would seem to require at least the ability to read and explain any selection from the text of Torah. This makes most sense if we recognize the *mitzvah*'s interest in guaranteeing a basic cultural knowledge among Jews, the knowledge of the word of God vouchsafed to us.

That is certainly not an upper limit, and the Talmud conspicuously includes in its discussion of the *mitzvah* stories of people who came to know the entire expanse of Torah-related literature, but that does not affect the basic obligation. All the rest of what people study — Talmud, commentaries, codes, etc. — serves to enrich our understanding of the original document and how to apply it in practice to this world.

Autonomous Choices Inherent in the *Mitzvah* of *Talmud Torah*

Those aspects of the *mitzvah* show the necessity of making personal choices at almost each step of its observance. Fathers will have to make individual choices as to how to best help each son absorb the lessons he needs; as *Mishlei* says חנוך לנער על פי דרכו educate the child in his own way.[23] While one boy might be ready for a full day of study at a young age, others will need a more

---

22. See Rashi, *Kiddushin* 30a, s.v. *Torah*, and Rambam, *Hilchot Talmud Torah* 1:7 and 1:12.

23. 22:6.

patient approach. The how of fulfilling this obligation is thus left up to each father (intentionally, I believe).[24]

Beyond that, people naturally achieve different levels of knowledge and/or focus on differing disciplines. While some will be intellectually and emotionally suited to deep knowledge of all of Torah, others will focus on specific areas.[25] Some learn best in one style, others another, and most are perfectly acceptable. As before, the *mitzvah* gives a basic universal minimum, leaving room for personal decisions and creativity.

We have several *mitzvot* to go in our project of unveiling the necessary self-determination in observance. *Halachic* literature defines the next one, Shabbat, so well that we might be fooled into thinking we can be satisfied by just adhering to those laws. We turn to that in the next chapter.

---

24. This also explains the Talmudic principle that courts need not interfere with minors who transgress the Torah. Since the child's education was left up to the father, courts cannot judge a particular minor's circumstances well enough to mix in.

25. In the nineteenth century, a man produced a forgery of the Jerusalem Talmud on the section dealing with sacrifices and Temple worship. He gathered rabbinic approbations for the work, fooling many Torah scholars into thinking it authentic. Supposedly, the Rogotchover spotted the forgery in that it did not mention any scholars unique to that tractate. In his mastery of Talmudic literature, he had noticed that aside from the giants whose names are all over the Talmud, there were always scholars who appeared only in a particular tractate. Apparently, their Torah skills had prepared them to contribute lastingly to that area of study, but not others. It is exactly this kind of individual interest and expertise that the *mitzvah* welcomes, another example of expecting Jews to autonomously choose how to build on the Torah's minimal obligations.

Chapter 18

Shabbat and Its Concern
with Positive Rest

The positive aspects of Shabbat are less well-developed in Jewish literature than the prohibitions, perhaps precisely because they are meant to be so personal. I believe I can show, however, that Shabbat was meant to be a day of soul-refreshing freedom from creativity, with prohibitions to foster the atmosphere of the day, not define it.

I cannot claim this is a universal view, since some important authorities seem to see the positive content of Shabbat as a side note to the prohibitions. While even this view knows the Torah couches the requirement to desist from creative labor as both a prohibition and an obligation, they see that as a way for the system to invest these rules with greater seriousness than just an ordinary prohibition. The author of *Sefer haChinuch*, for a prominent example, sees no new content in the positive form of the *mitzvah*, telling readers to consult his discussion of the prohibition.[1]

On the significant other hand, Rambam and Ramban saw the obligation as a religiously distinct requirement, and understood that positive content as the goal of the day. Rambam opens the 21st chapter of the Laws of Shabbat by mentioning that the Torah's use of the word תשבות, you shall rest,[2] requires desisting even from activities that do not fall under any *melachah* prohibition. He then spends the next several chapters listing rabbinically prohibited

---

1. See *Mitzvot* 85 and 32.
2. *Shemot* 23:12.

actions, many legislated only because they are similar to biblically proscribed ones.[3]

For Rambam, תשבות, you shall rest, taught the rabbis that the Torah wanted Jews to avoid activities that smack of creative labor, not just the ones that technically qualify as such or carry the danger of leading to a transgression. He read the Talmudic presentation to mean that the Torah-ordained prohibited labors established categories from which to desist on Shabbat; while only those particular labors incur capital liability, the intent was that Jews would refrain from those and similar activities. The rabbis defined the Torah's wishes more explicitly.

Ramban ordinarily disagrees with Rambam about how to understand the Talmud's declaration that a certain *mitzvah* encompasses both an obligation and a prohibition. While Rambam will codify two *mitzvot* in such circumstances, Ramban will not.[4] In our reading of what positive obligations add to prohibitions, Ramban would be saying that the Torah does not always mean to add religious content when it enacts a separate positive requirement.

Here, whatever the technical issues, Ramban notes that the Torah commanded Jews to make the day a שבתון, a word he defines (for both Shabbat and holidays) as obligating rest — in the ordinary sense of the word — in addition to the technical laws

---

3. This is different than prohibiting an action because it might lead to a biblically prohibited one; that would be protective, whereas Rambam is speaking of the Shabbat laws as a framework, not a final definition. For an example, see *Hilchot Shabbat* 22:23, which codifies a rabbinic prohibition against coloring one's face because it was similar to painting or dyeing. It seems unlikely that the rabbis worried that putting color on one's face would lead to painting or dyeing an animal hide. Rather, the prohibition told the rabbis that that kind of activity did not belong on Shabbat, so they named other activities that are inappropriate by extension.

4. See his gloss to the sixth of Rambam's introductory principles to the *Sefer haMitzvot*.

of avoiding creative labor.[5] In his view, this was to insure that the day not become one of labor that the prohibitions did not cover, such as moving furniture inside one's house.

Positive Rest and Its Centrality

A verse that figures prominently in the Shabbat liturgy suggests that this positive rest is central to our experience of the day. The Torah speaks of "observing" Shabbat, "ושמרו בני ישראל את השבת, לעשות את השבת לדורותם ברית עולם, the Children of Israel shall observe the Shabbat, to make the Shabbat in all their generations, an eternal covenant."[6] The verb troubled commentators, since there is no *making*, no constitutive element to the prohibitions. I suggest the Torah was signaling that the prohibitions only lay the groundwork; we "make" Shabbat with our positive rest.

That also explains the Talmud's assumption that if women are included in the prohibitions, the obligations must apply to them as well, that "anyone included in שמור (the word used in the second Decalogue; for the Talmud, it refers to prohibitions) is included in זכור (from the first Decalogue, taken to refer to *Kiddush* and other obligations of the day)."[7]

Unless there is a deep connection between the prohibitions and obligations, we would have to see this היקש, this informative juxtaposition, as completely technical. If the prohibitions are preparatory to proper observance of the active obligation of rest, though, the juxtaposition tells us something. Since the prohibitions are there to guide us in achieving the desired positive state

---

5. See his interpretation of the word in *Vayikra* 23:24 and his *Sermon for Rosh haShanah*, printed in *Kitvei Ramban*, ed. C. Chavel (Mossad haRav Kook: Jerusalem, 1968). Note that the Talmudic prohibition of feeding wild animals on Shabbat because of the effort involved, *Shabbat* 155b, also points towards an expectation that Jews would not exert themselves on Shabbat except as necessary.
6. *Shemot* 31:16.
7. *Berachot* 20b.

of rest, one who is required to adhere to those prohibitions must obviously be included in the obligations.

Rashi's explanation of a strange Talmudic requirement for a person who loses track of the days of the week provides one last proof that Shabbat should really be about the positive experience. In the course of the discussion,[8] the Talmud assumes that on *every* day of that person's life, until he or she rediscovers the actual date for Shabbat, such a person can only do as much Shabbat-prohibited labor as necessary to maintain life, since that day *might* be Shabbat. Nonetheless, the Talmud requires the person to treat one day a week as *actually* Shabbat, which the Talmud defines as reciting *Kiddush* and *Havdallah*, verbalizations of the Jew's recognition of the advent and departure of Shabbat.

Rashi explains that the recitations are symbolic, to insure the person not completely forget Shabbat. Considering that this person is daily refraining from anything other than life-sustaining labor, that claim seems difficult; would a person who daily must restrict his or her activities because it might be Shabbat possibly forget the concept? I think the comment shows that Rashi understood the Talmud to see *Kiddush, Havdallah*, and other positive expressions of the day as the essence of the Shabbat experience.

What Makes for a Positive Experience?

The stress on the positive in these sources does not enlighten us as to how they should look. *Kiddush* and *Havdallah* may define the chronological boundaries of the day, but they cannot be the whole picture. Two further seemingly technical pieces of information about the prohibited labors of Shabbat suggest an answer that also shows how Shabbat observance has to be personally defined.

Although the Torah defines the cessation of labor as imitating God's "resting" on the seventh day of Creation, tradition assumes the specific categories of prohibited labor come from the construction of the *Mishkan*, the Tabernacle built in the desert as

---

8. *Shabbat* 69a.

a proto-Temple.[9] The relationship between the two creations is never fully explained, but the Talmud seems to assume the building of the *Mishkan* is the height of human imitation of God's creation; the activities that make the list, then, are those that bring a person closest to the Divine standard of making the world.

The second technicality, the rule of חילוק מלאכות, that each Shabbat violation can be punished on its own, shows that each of these acts independently destroys the Shabbat experience. The rule states that violating any of these types of labor incurs separate liability; in contrast to a holiday, a person who — without full recognition of what he or she was doing wrong — both plowed and cooked on Shabbat would be liable for two sacrifices. Unwitting violations *within* a category, such as cooking, baking, and frying, obligate only one sacrifice. Not each *act* of Shabbat violation is punishable, but each *type* of act.[10]

The rule makes sense only if each category has independent meaning and importance. Were Shabbat just a composite created by observing various prohibitions, violating one should be no different than violating another, and the rule should be either that all acts can be covered by one sacrifice or that each act requires a separate one.

The centrality of category distinguishes "rest" on Shabbat from the ordinary meaning of the word. In addition to ordinary rest, as Ramban pointed out, חילוק מלאכות shows us Shabbat was a conscious retreat from certain kinds of effort. It is not only that we do not act in these ways, we are meant to be conscious of each

---

9. See, for example, *Shabbat* 49b. There are significant debates as to whether the categories built only off those actions necessary for the construction of the *Mishkan* or even its continued functioning, as well as the question of whether the purpose of these acts is defined by the purpose for which they were used in the *Mishkan*. Each of these, of course, would slightly affect the presentation in the text, but need not be fully elaborated here.

10. See *Shabbat* 70a, with Rashi, s.v. *Hilluk Melachot*.

type of way in which we are not acting.[11] Rest involves deliberate retreat from certain kinds of effort.

The *Imitatio Dei* of Shabbat Rest

This also explains how we imitate God in desisting from these labors. The Torah tells us that God created the world in six days and ceased on Shabbat, adding the word וינפש. Rashi and Ibn Ezra translate that word as "and He revived Himself," which is philosophically problematic, as Ibn Ezra notes.[12]

Perhaps those problems led the kabbalists to connect the extra word, וינפש, to the word for the soul, נפש, and see this as a reference to a נשמה יתירה, an extra soul, that inhabits a Jew over the course of Shabbat.[13] Ramban also records the kabbalistic view that Shabbat maintains the soul, although he does not explore how that happens.[14]

The attentive breaking off of creative activity would be one way. Creativity, in all forms, cannot be continuous; bursts of activity depend on periods of contraction and criticism, where the creator (and/or others) analyze the work that has been performed, fully absorbing what has been achieved.[15] Used as a time to consciously, actively, and thoughtfully step away from the week's various modes of creativity, Shabbat lays the groundwork for even more productive creativity in the week to come. The rejuvenation feeds the creativity; it is not separate from it.

---

11. Prescribing sacrificial atonement for transgressions that lacked full knowledge implies some fault in the person's ignorance. For Shabbat, that would mean we are obligated to be aware of each of these categories throughout the day; that forgetting is no excuse shows that part of Shabbat is the active awareness of desisting from each of the categories.
12. *Shemot* 31:17.
13. See, for example, Ramban's comment on *Shemot* 31:13.
14. Commentary to *Bereshit* 2:7.
15. As Matthew Arnold noted, in his essay, "On the Function of Criticism at the Present Time," referenced frequently by *mori ve-rabi* R. Aharon Lichtenstein.

Applying verses to God always involves difficult anthropomorphisms, but seeing *va-yinafash* as referring to an active rest that sets up the next period of creativity offers a palatable reading. It does not mean that God rejuvenated Himself, an abhorrent idea, but that God stepped back from His most active involvement in Creation for a period of review and consideration. Shabbat for people seeks the same kind of active review, in which the person considers how he or she created in the week gone by, learning the lessons of the past before embarking on the future.

As soon as we see Shabbat as internally productive, however, it necessarily must adapt to and be adapted by each person. A farmer will experience his stoppage of creative labor differently than a construction foreman or a scribe. In each case, the laws of the day are the same, but the resulting experience is and should be individualized.

This is not exactly true of the holidays, as we will see next chapter, but we stop to rest and creatively absorb what we have seen so far, so many observances that are important, vital, and central to Jewish experience, and yet leave much of the content of that experience up to the individual Jew.

Chapter 19

The Personal Element in the Holidays, Charity, and Honoring Parents

In many senses, the holidays are all the same. For example, the rules for desisting from creativity, different than those for Shabbat, are the same for all the major holidays, allowing the kinds of labor, known as מלאכת אוכל נפש, activity that sustains the soul.

But other components differentiate them; *Pesach* celebrates the Exodus and the beginning of the harvest season, *Shavuot* reminds us of the offering of the שתי הלחם, the two loaves of bread that are the first sacrifices from that year's wheat harvest and occurs on or around the anniversary of the Giving of the Torah at Sinai, and *Sukkot* marks both the completion of the harvest and commemorates God's protecting us in the desert.

Separate Commandments, Separate Rests

Interestingly, Rambam separately counts the commandment to rest on each holiday, where he might have grouped them as one, "to desist from creative labor that is not soul-sustaining on the various holidays." At the same time, he *does* include the seventh day of Passover in the general commandment of that holiday, showing us that it is not each *day* of rest that gets a separate *mitzvah*, it is each *holiday's* rest, despite their *halachic* identity.

I claim that this differentiates the kind of rest expected as well. Before realizing this, we might think the holidays' differences from each other are fully revealed by the מצוות היום, the commandments of each day. The requirement to sit in booths on *Sukkot*, for example, tells us something about the day; it is important to note, though, that it does not cover all of one's actions over the course of the day. It would be mistaken, therefore, to see the sitting in the *sukkah* or the telling of the Exodus story as the *entirety* of a day's import, but it provides information as to what the day itself is supposed to look like.

The traditional liturgy offers a complementary avenue to fleshing out the content of these special days, in the descriptions we give when we name them in our prayers. In both the *Amidah*, the standing prayer, and the Grace After Meals of these days, we find *Pesach* called זמן חרותנו, the time of our freedom, *Shavuot* זמן מתן תורתנו, the time of the giving of the Torah, and *Sukkot* זמן שמחתנו, the time of our happiness.

Last chapter, I suggested that *halachic* rest is actually a stepping back from creativity to absorb lessons learned and to prepare for the next burst of creativity. Applying that here, we can see why the experience should differ on each holiday as well. The lessons we are to absorb from stepping back on a holiday of freedom likely differ from those we learn in the context of receiving the Torah (or renewing our Godly service in the Temple), and yet again from that same rest in the context of remembering how God can and does protect and provide for us.

As before, the laws set up only a basic and universally applicable guideline for the kinds of experience being sought; the task of fleshing that experience out fully is left to the autonomous choices of each Jew.

To Give Charity

There are many ways to show the role of personal insight and understanding in shaping one's fulfillment of the *mitzvah* of giving charity, but I will focus on two. First, common parlance might lead us to believe that donating money to any worthy cause qualifies as צדקה, charity, but the Talmudic sources and their resulting codification in the *Shulchan Aruch* concentrate more directly on the poor and their needs.[1]

There are many other good causes as well, such as Jewish education, building synagogues and houses of study, supporting medical research, visiting the sick, comforting the bereaved, and a host of others. Some of those also fit the rubric of helping the poor, such as by noting that the poor can certainly not pay for their medical care, and especially not for diseases whose cure is still unknown or experimental. Supporting medical research, in that context, might qualify as charity in the helping-the-poor sense.

Too, the common custom to give at least ten percent of one's income to charity might not be restricted to charity in the technical sense, charity for the poor. Nonetheless, the plethora of causes and their relationship to essential charity show some of the challenges of using our money appropriately, even with all good will. Some will choose to give ten percent, some more, some less. Within those monies, too, there will be a range of choices to be made about apportioning; while traditional sources offer some guidance, much is left to the individual.

Rambam famously lists eight levels of charity, collated from various Talmudic discussions.[2] The highest of those levels, the best fulfillment of the obligation, is to support another Jew or righteous non-Jew before that person's financial situation deteriorates so much as to need actual alms.

The possible ways to accomplish this include giving a gift, making a loan, forging a partnership with the needy person, or finding him some other source of livelihood. Each of these strategies calls for complex calculations of how to best steady a person teetering on the edge of the underclass. Since Rambam assumes the *mitzvah* applies to the near-poor as well as the already-poor,

---

1. For some examples, see *Bava Batra* 8a-11a and שו״ע י״ד (*Yoreh Deah*) 247ff.
2. *Hilchot Matnot Aniyim* 10:7–14.

the number and kinds of choices to be made are multiplied, without any specific rules for how to make those choices.

The person intent on giving charity in the best way possible, we now find, must make significant personal decisions at each stage. First, he or she must decide whether to give to the poor or other worthy causes (or what percentage to give to each kind of cause). Within the amount being given to a particular type of cause, the donor must identify recipients, choosing among the candidates, and deciding how to divide the funds. Even once those decisions have been reached, the donor must further decide whether to give by outright gift, loan, partnership, or finding the person employment. None of these choices is simple; each of them is largely a personal and autonomous matter, but the end result will change the quality of one's charity considerably.

Honoring and Fearing Parents

While the commandments of honor and fear are obviously related, the Torah separates them, placing כבוד, honor, in the עשרת הדברות, the Sinai statements known as the Ten Commandments, and leaving יראה, fear, for the beginning of *Vayikra* 18. In seeking the balance between the well-defined and that left to the individual conscience, I will also try to explain both why the Torah would present them so separately, especially when works such as the *Sefer haMitzvot* and *Shulchan Aruch*[3] juxtapose them.

Although כבוד is always translated as "honor," the Talmud defines it as specific services the child must perform, מאכיל ומשקה, מלביש ומכסה, מכניס ומוציא, giving (the parent) food and drink, covering and clothing, taking in and out. The list implies that "honor" refers to caring for a parent's physical needs.

The obligation of יראה, awe or fear, complements "honor." The Talmud defines "fear" as not sitting or standing in the parent's place, not speaking before, contradicting, calling by his/her first name (or, if the name is unusual, calling someone *else* by that

---

3. *Sefer haMitzvot*, Positive Commands 210 and 211, and *Yoreh Deah* 240.

name), and not wading into a debate in which a parent is partaking, even to support the parent's point of view. These imply that a child is supposed to view the parent with a certain amount of fear or awe, simply stated; indeed, Rambam says the *mitzvah* is to act towards the parent as towards someone with the power to administer meaningful punishment. It should be obvious that the fear is not in and of itself the Torah's goal, so that here, too, we are prodded to look deeper into the *mitzvah*.

Representing the Divine

Here is where we come to the point I raised earlier in the context of the Noahides, that the Talmud understands Scripture to make a conscious parallel between the terms used for these *mitzvot* and the prescribed attitude towards God.[4] Thus, the verse warns *kabed* (honor) parents, and elsewhere says *kabed* God; so, too, it warns איש אמו ואביו תיראו, every one of you must fear his mother and father, and את ה׳ אלוקיך תירא, fear the Lord your God. The use of similar terms, the rabbis imply, indicates our attitude towards our parents should parallel that towards God. As two of the three partners in making a baby, parents have standing akin to that of the third, the Creator.[5]

Recognizing that these commandments stem from parents' role as creators also fits the *Sefer haChinuch*'s assertion that this *mitzvah* inculcates gratitude, which he explicitly assumes will increase the person's gratitude to God as well. The honoring of parents thus only partially cares about securing them their due; they also serve as a convenient vehicle to personalize our relationship with our Creator.

Rambam's phrasing of two more rules supports this idea. *Halachah* prohibits restraining one's parent (verbally or physically), even if the parent is embarrassing or otherwise causing distress to the child. In an extreme example, a child may not

---

4. *Kiddushin* 30b.
5. The image appears in the Talmud, ibid.

stop a parent from throwing a bag full of money into the ocean.[6] Rambam highlights the relationship to God by ruling that the child seeing such a parent throw the money away must "sit silently and accept the decree of Scripture." Similarly, he writes that the child may not answer back if the parent embarrasses him publicly, but must maintain his fear of the King of Kings.

Note that his justification in both cases relies on the child's obligations towards God, not towards the parent. The goal is to see this physical person as parallel to God, to use that as a stepping-stone to inculcating a more full honor and fear of God.

This perspective of the commandments of honor and awe also shows us where the personal element enters the picture, completely unguided by specific laws. Alongside the codified laws, the Talmud gives numerous examples of admirable respect or fear of one's parents. Perhaps most famously, Dama b. Netina is commended for refusing to wake his father, who was sleeping on the key to a cabinet that held merchandise he could have sold right then for an extraordinary profit.[7] Since Dama was not even Jewish, the Talmud could not have meant his example as *halachically* instructive; rather, it meant it as evincing an ideal to strive to actualize.

Kibbud expresses this aspect even more fully. While a child could treat the obligations completely technically, ensuring only that the parent eats, drinks, is clothed, and gets out regularly, the responsibilities of *kibbud* seem to call for broader involvement in assuring that the parent's needs are met. If so, the Torah places the more easily and exactly defined obligation, awe or fear, in a legal section of the Torah. Honor, the broader and more personally defined responsibility, is placed in the Ten Commandments.

In sum, eight *mitzvot* show us how poorly an overreliance on codified *halachah* serves the Jew trying to fulfill the Torah. Although they define goals, we have seen how general the

---

6. Rambam, *Hilchot Mamrim* 6:7. Others, noting that the obligation of honor does not extend to the child's using his own money, disagree.
7. *Kiddushin* 31a.

guidelines can be, even in the most central *mitzvot*. In each of these cases (and I could add many others), full success requires the individual Jew to build off of *halachah*'s guidelines in defining how he or she fulfills the obligation in question.

Chapter 20

Autonomy as a Key to Understanding Women's Lesser Obligation in *Mitzvot*

In the first part, I noted that Rambam's presentation of the sixty *mitzvot* that shape an ordinary male life offered two perspectives of women's lesser list of such obligations. Now that we have spent some time seeing how significant personal autonomy is to religiosity, we can make some of those points more fully.

In recent decades, we have witnessed a wholesale rethinking of women's roles in society, including religion. Some of that has redounded to the good of all, enriching society as a whole. In Judaism, that process has also uncovered areas of sensitivity, where the religion seems to relegate women to a role they find restrictive or dismissive.

One particular such area has been the unequal levels of obligation between men and women, the fact of women's exemption from many *mitzvot*. Those exemptions lead women to feel excluded, both from public worship (where their exemption means they cannot take on certain roles, such as blowing *shofar* for the congregation) and from central private *mitzvot* such as the study of Torah or wearing *tefillin*.

For many of these women, the fact that they *may* fulfill these commandments is insufficient, since they are still being told, as they hear it, that Judaism either cares less about their relationship with God, or does not imagine that women are capable of building such a relationship as well as men.

A Different Lens: A More Autonomous Religiosity

In the light of our discussion, I think we have room for a new look at women's exemption from many מצוות עשה שהזמן גרמא — positive commandments with a time element to them. Doing so will, I hope, further our understanding of the importance of personal input to one's relationship with God, while also fortifying our sense that Judaism values women's religious development as much as men's.

The first step is remembering that specificity of obligation is not as significant a value for the Torah as we might have thought. Not being included in certain obligations excludes women in one way — they cannot be agents of fulfillment of that *mitzvah*, as we mentioned — but might leave them with an equally valuable result, a greater autonomy to shape their service of God as they see fit. Especially since we've seen that God gave commandments only once human beings failed to use their autonomy the right way, women's freer religiosity need not carry the bite it often does.

This suggestion differs, I hope, from the well-known, roundly rejected argument that women did not need certain *mitzvot* because of their greater innate spirituality or because other *mitzvot* already trained them sufficiently. As I have argued elsewhere,[1] there is no obvious evidence that women are naturally better at serving God or reason to believe that a woman's obligations regarding her monthly cycle should teach her about seasonal *mitzvot* such as *sukkah* or *shofar*.

My argument instead is that the category of positive, time-related *mitzvot*, מצוות עשה שהזמן גרמא, establishes specific acts of worship, not general categories of religiosity. Since those acts all support broader goals — goals in which women *are* fully and equally obligated — women's exemption does not leave them out of anything of significance to the religion. Rather, while men are

---

1. "Men's and Women's Differing Religious Experiences, as Taught by the Category of *Mitzvot Aseh She-haZman Grama*" (Winter 2002) in *Women in Judaism* (*www.women-in-judaism.com*).

guided more specifically in how to achieve a proper religiosity, women are left with greater freedom as to how to shape their religiosity.

Exemption is Not Exclusion: The Availability of These *Mitzvot*

I should also pause to stress the difference between exemption and exclusion. Women often feel that they are "left out" of these *mitzvot*. Were the *mitzvot* in question essential to the religion, or were there no other way to secure reward, exemption would in fact equal exclusion. If not, the difference remains crucial; women *may* use these acts to foster a relationship with God but need not see them as the only path to that goal.

Complicating the picture, Jewish men *do* experience these rituals as definitive of their religiosity, seemingly justifying women's sense that they are being discriminated against. For men, acts such as saying Shema twice a day, wearing *tsitsit* and *tefillin*, shaking a *lulav* on *Sukkot*, and counting the Omer between *Pesach* and *Shavuot* are *the* markers of their religiosity, how they define themselves as observant. Judging from men, truly serving God necessarily involves these acts.

I hope we have seen enough to already spot the error in this perspective. First, we have seen that men overemphasize the centrality of these *mitzvot*; most of them are, in fact, specific expressions of broader religious ideals, with the underlying ideals the real point. Rather than ends of their own, these *mitzvot* are tools to a broader goal. Women, in each case, were exempted only from the specific acts, not the goals.

Defining the Exempt Category

That leads to another question, why the system required these acts of men but not women. The Talmud's derivation of this exemption, it is already interesting to point out, makes no broad claims about women, their nature, or their lack of appropriateness for these *mitzvot*. Rather, it cites verses, leaving to us the task of teasing out the verses' implicit messages.

When the Talmud mentions positive, time-related *mitzvot*, it provides a list we can use as the basis for our discussion. The Talmud says:[2]

ת"ר: איזוהי מצות עשה שהזמן גרמא? סוכה, ולולב, שופר, וציצית,
ותפילין; ואיזוהי מצות עשה שלא הזמן גרמא? מזוזה, מעקה, אבידה,
ושילוח הקן. וכללא הוא? הרי מצה, שמחה, הקהל, דמצות עשה שהזמן
גרמא, ונשים חייבות! ותו, והרי תלמוד תורה, פריה ורביה, ופדיון הבן,
דלאו מצות עשה שהזמן גרמא הוא, ונשים פטורות! אמר רבי יוחנן: אין
למדין מן הכללות ואפילו במקום שנאמר בו חוץ, ...

Our rabbis learned: What are positive commandments with a time element? *Sukkah, lulav, shofar, tsitsit*, and *tefillin*; and what are positive *mitzvot* without any element of time? *Mezuzah, ma'akeh* [building a fence around any elevated platform], *avedah* [returning lost objects], and *shiluah ha-kan* [sending away the mother before removing babies from a nest]. Is it a general rule? Look at *matsah, simchah* [celebrating on holidays], and *hakhel* [the national gathering on *Sukkot* after the *shemittah* year], positive commandments with a time component, and women are obligated! In addition, look at Torah study, procreation, and redeeming a firstborn son, which are not positive commandments with a time component, yet women are exempt! Said R. Yohanan: We do not rely [completely] on general rules, even where the rule was stated with some exceptions...

Before we take up the *mitzvot* that populate the list, we should spend a moment on the name given to this category. Calling these *mitzvot* "commandments that time causes" seems to ignore the minimal time component in some of them. The time aspect of *sukkah* or *shofar* is clear — they come around once a year

---

2. *Kiddushin* 33b-34a.

— but *tsitsit* and *tefillin* are time related only in a more tenuous sense.[3]

Indeed, the Talmud recognizes that some opinions would exclude *tefillin* from this list, because they hold they can be worn on Shabbat and at night.[4] Those who do include *tefillin* — and, as we will see, use it as the *source* for women's exemption — assume that *tefillin*'s not being worn on Sabbaths and holidays suffices to consider the *mitzvah* "caused by time." So, too, *tsitsit* make the list because the *mitzvah* applies during the day but not at night (although it does apply *every* day). The Talmud does not explain how that justifies the term "שהזמן גרמא, which time caused." Deciphering the term would seem crucial to understanding the category and its implications.

Beyond that, the numerous exceptions make the whole insistence that there is a category striking; women are obligated in some *mitzvot* despite their being time-related, and exempt from others despite their *not* being time-related.[5] I suggest the positing of the category captures some truth about what the Torah meant in terms of women's observance, although that truth is not immediately obvious.

The Subsidiary Status of Time-Related *Mitzvot*

Almost the only clear connection among all these *mitzvot* is their being explicitly joined to a broader religious idea. Sitting in a *sukkah,* for example, is meant to contribute to the atmosphere of the holiday, not to stand alone as an act of worship of God. This is clear in the verse that establishes the requirement, which tells us to do so, "למען ידעו דורותיכם כי בסכות הושבתי את בני ישראל בהוציאי אותם

---

3. See, e.g., *Kiddushin* 29a, s.v. אותו, where Tosafot assume that being applicable only by day suffices to render a *mitzvah* time related. In the question, Tosafot entertained the possibility that only starting at the eighth day of life would also suffice for membership in the category.

4. *Kiddushin* 35a, with the sources mentioned by Rashi.

5. That the whole distinction is assumed to apply only to positive commandments is itself suggestive.

מארץ מצרים, so that your generations should know that I caused the Jews to reside in tents when I took them out of Egypt."[6]

The verse does not mean we should remember God's kindnesses to us in the desert only when actually inside that temporary residence; it intends the holiday as a whole to inculcate and fortify that awareness, with the act of living in the *sukkah* one obligatory avenue to that goal. Even for men, the Torah could have set up the holiday without such practices and still expected us to remember that aspect of the Exodus.

Shofar fits this model as well. Although many experience it as central to Rosh haShanah (with the rest of the day a little blank) and the Torah refers to the holiday as a whole as a *day* of blowing (as *Sukkot* is a holiday of booths),[7] the requirement, by Torah law, is only to hear nine *shofar* blasts at some point during the day.[8] Further, there is no obligation or preference that a Jew *blow*, only that he *hear* a *shofar* blown.

As with *Sukkot*, it would seem odd to say that nine blasts completely or essentially capture the goals of the day. Rather, blowing the *shofar* is supposed to shape the rest of the day by reminding us of its nature. While women need not participate in the blowing,

---

6. *Vayikra* 23:43. The plainest sense of the text seems to apply that reason for the taking of the *Arba Minim*, the Four Species, as well, although many explain that obligation as related to the harvest aspect of the holiday. Either way, *lulav* is almost always seen as reflecting a deeper idea, not an end of its own.

7. A זכרון תרועה or a יום תרועה; see *Vayikra* 23:24 and *Bamidbar* 29:1. In *Vayikra*, Ramban assumes that the "memory" is that which is caused by our *shofar*-blowing.

8. Two factors lead to our hearing many more blasts than that, a confusion about how to blow a *teruah*, see *Rosh haShanah* 33b, and an attachment to the number one hundred, based on an assertion of the sixteenth-century R. Isaiah Horowitz (Shelah). Placing *shofar* blowing in Musaf, almost universally assumed to be rabbinic, gives it more centrality to the day's liturgy than the Torah itself required. I focus on the Torah's demands because only that is relevant to understanding why the Torah exempted women.

they are equally obligated to experience the יום תרועה, the Holiday of Blowing.

Similarly, Shema is a twice-daily reminder of truths we are separately required to believe, recited or not; a Jew who did not have the *mitzvah* of Shema would still need to actively believe all the truths contained therein. The counting of the Omer from *Pesach* to *Shavuot* is a specific act, but one meant to foster an awareness of the connections between the two holidays; the counting helps insure we are fully aware of what is occurring during that time.

Once we see that women were only exempted from mandated expressions of ideas and beliefs incorporated in other commandments, we have room to suggest God left women free to choose their path towards those larger goals. This would then fit well with my general theme, that personal autonomy is an important part of Jewish religiosity, and may be more prominent in the case of women than men.

That does not fully explain the exemption, for two reasons. First, women *are* obligated in other similarly subsidiary *mitzvot*, such as *mezuzah*, forcing us to explain the difference between time-related *mitzvot* and others. More significantly, we need to consider why the Torah would allow women greater freedom (as opposed to men), and why it would express that freedom in terms of this category of *mitzvot*.

Go To the Source

On questions like these, the way the Talmud arrived at an idea is often as instructive as the conclusion it reaches. In our case, the Talmud's analysis of women's exemption from these *mitzvot* makes several revealing points: (1) Those authorities who saw *tefillin* as time-related (as we do for *halachic* purposes)[9] also saw it as the source of women's exemption from *all* time-related

---

9. The Talmud knows of those who think *tefillin* can be worn at night and on Shabbat; for them, *tefillin* is not time-related.

mitzvot. (2) The Talmud infers women's exemption from *tefillin*'s having been twice juxtaposed to the obligation to transmit Torah from one generation to the next (*Talmud Torah*). (3) That *mitzvah* — to teach Torah to our children — is one of two positive commandments without a time component from which women are nonetheless exempt.

The oddity in that derivation deserves a moment's thought. *Tefillin*'s exemption is carried over to the rest of the category, which would seem to mean it is typical, yet its own exemption is derived from its scriptural proximity to a *mitzvah* from the other category, and an exception at that. It is almost as if the Talmud is signaling to us that the category of positive, time-related commandments shares a significant characteristic with the obligation to study Torah, despite the latter's not having any significant time component. The derivation of women's exemption from Torah study should therefore shed light on our category as well.

The focal point of the Talmud's discussion there is the Scriptural phrase that establishes a father's obligation to transmit knowledge of at least the Written Torah to his sons, ולמדתם אותם את בניכם, you shall teach them to your children. Since the obligation is parental, the Talmud first wants a source exempting women from having to pass on such knowledge to their sons, and points to the first word of the phrase. While we read that word as *ve-limadtem*, and you shall teach, those letters as written in the Torah could signify the word *u-lemadtem*, and you shall learn. Because of this ambiguity, the Talmud sees the Torah as signaling that only a parent personally obligated to study bears the obligation to teach.

Then, to prove that mothers need not study on their own, the Talmud reverses the readings above, noting that while the word *could* be read as *u-lemadtem*, it is actually read as *ve-limadtem*, teaching that only people whose parent(s) had to teach them need to study themselves. To close the circle, the Talmud notes that we know a father is not required to teach his daughters (which, as we have just seen, implies that the daughter need not study on her own, nor teach her sons), because the verse says "your sons," which Talmudic tradition knew meant the exclusion of daughters.[10]

The Surprise Nature of the *Mitzvah* of *Talmud Torah* — Guaranteeing the Chain

As we saw earlier, here, too, the Torah stresses the aspect of transmission in the *mitzvah* of Torah study, emphasizing its linkage to the experience of being taught and of teaching others. Only a child whose parent bore an obligation to teach must study on his own — either to replace or supplement the parent's teaching — and pass that study on to the next generation. Others may study as much or as little as they want, but are not responsible for ensuring the continuity of this chain of transmission.

Putting this together with the fact that the minimum requirement of Torah study encompasses only the Written Torah, we are reminded that the most stripped-down version of the *mitzvah* of *Talmud Torah* seeks to insure that a segment of the Jewish people will know the basic texts of the religion and pass on that knowledge. I emphasize this both because it differs sharply from the way the *mitzvah* is generally presented and also because it is crucial to understanding why God might have chosen not to impose that same obligation and responsibility upon another segment of the population, women.

I have mentioned that the minimum obligation is to know the Written Torah, which Rashi saw as the Five Books of the Torah, while Rambam included all of Tanach. Compared to the goal of knowing all of Torah, which seems to be the ideal fulfillment of the *mitzvah*, this minimum might seem rather light.

In the real world, however, it is extraordinarily difficult to ensure that each male Jew achieves meaningful knowledge of even

---

10. *Kiddushin* 29b. The Torah's references to sons do not always mean males exclusively; one clear example would be *Shemot* 13:8, והגדת לבנך ביום ההוא לאמור, and you shall tell your son on that day saying, a *mitzvah* that Rambam and *Sefer haChinuch* assume includes women.

just the חמשה חומשי תורה, the Pentateuch. I believe that a majority of male Orthodox Jews today have not achieved such knowledge, or have lost it through neglect and their failure to observe the rabbinic requirement to read the weekly Torah reading twice in the text and once in an authoritative translation.[11]

The Talmud itself was aware of the challenges involved in ensuring that children learn that which is required. The Talmud noted seemingly contradictory traditions as to how intensively to educate a boy, one referring to "stuffing it into him like an ox," the other to struggling with him in a way that even carries the threat of real suffering if the son refuses to study.[12]

The answer, that the first happens at age six, the second at twelve, interests me less than the assumption that education can become a battle of wills. That struggle seems foreign to us because much of the world, including the Jewish community, refuses to engage in it. Many insist that the experience of learning, including Torah study, be inviting and pleasant, Talmudic statements notwithstanding.

There may be sociological reasons to adjust our vision of how to bring about the required result — starving children to coerce their cooperation would be frowned upon by the authorities, let alone by Jewish society — but there is no reason to suspect the *mitzvah* has changed. The obligation of *Talmud Torah* is not to regularly perform the act of Torah study; it is for each

---

11. Rejuvenating our involvement with the text of Torah would have many positive effects, not least being that it would ease the endeavor of securing silence during public Torah readings.

12. *Ketubbot* 50a. The phrase is obscure, and used in only one other *halachic* context in the Talmud, *Kiddushin* 28a, where one person calls another a *rasha*, an evildoer. Here, Rashi understands the Talmud to be permitting the father to strap the son and to withhold his food until he studies. In *Kiddushin*, Rashi only allows hating the other, but seems to also allow working to minimize his business and even to deprive him of a livelihood. In *Bava Metzia* 71a, Rashi rejects the second half of that interpretation, specifically because there is no such possibility in the case of a father and son.

adult male Jew to himself know, and ensure that each of his sons knows, at least the Written Torah and as much else of Torah as possible.

Rigidity and Women

It is the rigidly defined nature of success in this *mitzvah*, I believe, that led to women's exemption, and that explains their similar exemption in positive, time-related *mitzvot*. The *mitzvah* of *Talmud Torah* makes more significant and more rigid demands than the ordinary positive commandments. Regardless of a person's proclivities, strengths, and weaknesses, knowledge of the Written Torah is *absolutely required*; for many male Jews, that is no mean feat and is often, sadly, a *mitzvah* quite simply neglected or ignored.

Similarly, the positive time-related *mitzvot* make specific and well-defined demands. Shema must be recited at certain times of day, a *shofar* must be blown on a certain day of the year, and so on. *Tefillin* and *tzitzit*, while not as obviously time-related, are nonetheless also extremely specific delineations of how to develop the relationship with God.

That rigidity is not as apparent in other obligations. We have seen that the positive sides of many other *mitzvot* are open to personal input as to how best to achieve them. Many of the more specific positive *mitzvot*, such as putting a *mezuzah* on one's door or fencing off one's roof, are situational; anyone who finds the burden onerous could choose not to enter into that situation.

The Talmud does not speak specifically about rigidity as the underlying issue, so I am speculating somewhat. The power of the idea, for me, lies in its ability to explain oddities of the Talmudic discussion. For example, using *tefillin* as the source of exemption is difficult if time is really the issue, given *tefillin*'s debatable and at best minimal connection to time. But the Talmudic experience of *tefillin* — worn at all times, including when encountering non-Jews — does make significant, specific, and fairly rigid demands; rather than a ritual appurtenance of prayer, the Talmud-experienced *tefillin* are an obligated aspect of self-presentation.[13]

Why Leave Women Out of the Obligation in Such *Mitzvot*?

Whether or not my suggestion so far has been convincing, I fear that readers will still insist that the rules discriminate. After all, men have been the most noticeable Jews in Jewish history, and for them, the study of Torah, wearing *tefillin*, sitting in a *sukkah*, and so on, constitute the backbone of religiosity. Arguing that those practices are not essential to a valid and productive relationship with God will strike many as apologetics unless I can explain why a God Who decided that Torah and *mitzvot* were necessary would also decide to exempt half of that nation from many parts of the system.

There may be many answers, but I will focus here on the easiest one to articulate, the importance of a balance between rigidity and flexibility. The Torah, as I understand it, stresses both obedient fidelity to God's command (where the goal is to fulfill what God said as exactly as possible) and the ability and readiness to express one's individuality within appropriate boundaries. While elements of that complex message are found within both men's and women's commandments, it is more effectively accomplished by having each of two groups emphasize one of the aspects.

In their relationship with God, men often strive to do exactly and only what God wants. Important and valuable where called for, that picture is only partial even for men. As I have been trying to show here, there are also occasions when God wants and demands our personal input and creativity. And yet my need to write this book suggests it is a message that can be easily lost.

---

13. *Berachot* 6a. Incidentally, viewing these exemptions as fostering a more personal religiosity offers another reason for the general *halachic* equation of women and partially converted slaves — they both need a freer version of the religion, although for very different reasons.

In my reading, women's greater religious freedom shows us a more individualized religiosity in action. Instead of all women studying Torah, for example, a healthy Jewish society would see women using their freer time to set more personalized agendas for how to become more God-like. Leaving women with greater choice offers the possibility that Jewish society as a whole will recognize the value and necessity of both sides of the equation — the response to specific commands in some situations and the personal journey towards God on the other, leaving individual Jews to find their place on the continuum between the two extremes.

But How Did God Choose Which Is Which?

I can answer this question technically or by appealing to essential differences between the two. Technically, women have always been more involved in the rearing of small children, a time that crucially needs freedom to develop in an individualized way as well as a calm acceptance of personal differences. While we certainly do not want to crush the individuality of adults, it is even more damaging to do so with small children. Helping those whom biology had set up as the caregivers for small children in their task would, to me, easily suffice as a reason for God to give them a freer form of the religion.

For those who do not mind claims about possible general differences between men and women, I also see room to suspect that women tend, on average, to prefer a less legalistic frame of mind, with more allowance for setting up their own rules, and taking account of individual differences.[14]

---

14. Many discussions of differences between men and women, without any connection to Judaism, support this claim. The work of Carol Gilligan, particularly *In a Different Voice*, points in this direction, as does that of Simon Baron-Cohen, who argues in his *The Essential Difference*, that, on average, men tend towards systems-building, towards understanding a set of rules for how something works and then applying those rules elsewhere, while women's minds tend towards empathy. If true, that would certainly justify establishing a more rigid system for men

I say that hesitantly; at an earlier stage of working through my thoughts on this issue, I mentioned my idea to a woman whose religious dedication I admired greatly. As I said it then, perhaps God did not define religiosity so rigidly for women because women bristle more than men at externally imposed character-izations, which they experience as an expression of authority. Ironically, she bristled at the idea!

As I bring my discussion of Talmudic evidence for a prefer-ence for personal insight and input into one's relationship with God to a close, many of my claims might seem uncomfortably innovative. That non-Jews have a positive role to play, depending only on their readiness to accept Judaism's worldview, that prayer is an opportunity for arguing with God about the best possible future, that *mitzvot* frequently require personal elaboration and delineation, and that women's exemption from a whole category is an example of a more general preference for individuation of one's relationship with God, all adopt positions not commonly discussed in Jewish circles. In the next chapter, I hope to show that important authorities have said this before.

(for them to understand and build on), leaving women more room to choose how to build their relationships (especially with God).

Chapter 21

Rambam, Ran, and the Importance of Personal Input Into Religion

The *Rishonim* Knew It, Too

Part of what encourages me in my views is that their basic thrust is found in numerous earlier writings. Here, I will discuss only two, Rambam and Ran, who approach Judaism from sharply different premises. Seeing that they agree about the importance of using one's own understandings to affect observance and religiosity will provide powerful support for the ideas I have offered.

Rambam's work is rife with comments that agree with my point, but two of his comments give extraordinary prominence to the religion's desire for each person's creative conceptualization of what it means to worship God. The first is about study of Torah, where Rambam is recording a Talmudic statement that says study should be divided equally between *Mikra*, Mishnah, and *Talmud* (although his text apparently read *gemara*, not *talmud*).[1] He interprets the first two terms as the Written and Oral Torah, Scripture and its interpretations, including the Talmudic and Geonic corpuses of law.

For the third, *gemara*, instead of naming a text to study (as we might expect from the first two entries on the list), Rambam writes:

...ושליש יבין וישכיל אחרית דבר מראשיתו ויוציא דבר מדבר וידמה דבר לדבר ויבין במדות שהתורה נדרשת בהן עד שידע היאך הוא עיקר המדות והיאך יוציא האסור והמותר וכיוצא בהן מדברים שלמד מפי השמועה, ועניין זה הוא הנקרא גמרא.

---

1. *Hilchot Talmud Torah* 1:11–12.

...and a third [of his time] he should understand and conceptualize the end of a matter from its beginning, deduce one matter from another, draw similarities among matters, and understand the rules by which the Torah is expounded until he knows the essence of those rules *and how to extract prohibited and permitted and the like from among the matters that were learned tradition-ally* [emphasis added], and this matter is called *gemara*.

Note that Rambam thinks the Talmud recommends we spend a full *third* of our Torah study time understanding the system's rules, to the point of being able to make independent yet accurate derivations of our own. In the following paragraph, he notes that more advanced students will spend almost *all* of their time on such efforts.

Knowing what to do, necessary as it is, is technical; Torah study, in Rambam's conception, aims much higher, at mastery of the system — the role of texts in that system, the role of tradi-tional assertions about proper practice — and how to coordinate the two. The highest level of understanding, as Rambam expresses it, is to know how to derive traditional facts of the *halachic* system creatively from Scripture.[2] In some areas — where *halachah* allows a later court to reach a different textual conclusion than an earlier one, a topic for another time — these derivations might even significantly alter Jewish practice.

Pardes and Where It Leads Us

In the next *halachah*, Rambam broadens the scope of expected

---

2. Ever since taking a course with Prof. Twersky, *a"h*, on the role of verses in Rambam's writings — and, I suspect, prodded by the kinds of preg-nant questions he would pose — I have often wondered whether this explains Rambam's noted tendency to offer source-verses other than those found in the Talmud. Rather than disagreeing with or ignoring the Talmud's derivation, he is demonstrating his own proficiency at creatively deriving ideas from Scripture.

creativity. He asserts that the topics known as *pardes* are included in the term *gemara*. Earlier,[3] he had defined *pardes* as מעשה בראשית and מעשה מרכבה, physics (the workings of the natural world) and metaphysics (the supernatural). His mentioning that such studies qualify as *gemara* conveys at least three startling pieces of information.

First, since *gemara* is more than just an understanding of facts, *pardes* must be as well. *Gemara* would lead a student to fully understand Scripture; how, when, and where texts were meant to lead to practical conclusions, and the nature of those conclusions. For *pardes*, that would suggest he means not only learning physics and metaphysics as known at a particular juncture in history, but developing deep comprehension of the workings of the universe, such that the person could creatively contribute to its shaping.[4]

Second, his including *pardes* in the *mitzvah* of Torah study seems to say that he saw studying the universe with an eye towards understanding the God Who created it as not only a fulfillment of the five *mitzvot* that have to do with loving and fearing Him, but as a performance of a central activity of Jewish worship, Torah study.

Finally, and most surprisingly, Rambam's comment means he did not limit the *mitzvah* of Torah study to the texts of the traditional canon. Torah study was not so much about study of Torah, it was about creative mastery of a certain type of information; while Torah contained that information, other "texts" did so as well, and the person who studied those other texts — although he or she would necessarily need a great deal of Torah background

---

3. *Hilchot Yesodei haTorah* 4:13.
4. In another pregnant question he left hanging, Professor Twersky *a"h* used to wonder aloud as to why Rambam placed these chapters at the beginning of his *halachic* work. I suspect Rambam's explicitly mentioning five *mitzvot* that the study of *pardes* fulfills, see *Hilchot Yesodei haTorah* 4:13, indicates he was trying to remind us that physics and metaphysics was not just another avenue to valuable truth, it was assumed by the Torah to be essential for the person of faith.

to properly approach the issue — could, with the right frame of mind, achieve a similar result.

Aside from what it reveals about this *mitzvah*, his comments problematize seeing *mitzvot* as ends of their own. Indeed, in promoting the achievement of reasonable mastery of *halachah* before moving on to *pardes*, Rambam reminds us of his view that knowledge of ordinary Torah topics "settles one's mind to begin with and also that they are the great good God supplied for the habitation of this world in order to inherit the World to Come, and they are knowable by all, small and great, man and woman, one of a broad heart and one of a narrow one."[5]

Right at the beginning of *Mishneh Torah*, then, Rambam stresses the importance of systematizing. God wanted people to understand the facts of the commandments, but also the underlying rules and principles. The measure of true success is the ability to arrive independently at correct new ideas about whichever system is under consideration.

The End of the Guide, in Both Meanings of the Word

Rambam's cryptic final comments to the *Guide for the Perplexed* seem to me also to point to a version of service of God that involves an enormous and little-recognized level of personal and autonomous input. In the last two chapters of the *Guide*, III:53 and 54, he defined four terms and four perfections. In chapter 53, he explains three of the terms, חסד משפט וצדקה — lovingkindness, justice, and righteousness — and explains how they can apply both to human beings and to God.

Chapter 54 opens with a discussion of the various meanings of the word חכמה, wisdom. Torah wisdom, for example, consists first of absorbing tradition, finding demonstrations and proofs for the Law, and finally of drawing inferences as to how to live, presumably in situations not covered by preceding cases (similar

---

5. *Hilchot Yesodei haTorah* 4:13.

to what we saw in Rambam's definition of *gemara*). He does not explain, up until this point, why he has defined these terms, nor does he tell us why he split the terms between chapters.

With the opening "After we have made all these preliminary remarks, hear what we shall say," he then introduces more definitions, now of the four human perfections: monetary, physical, moral, and the intellectual. Not surprisingly, Rambam sees that last perfection as higher than the others, terming it the "true human perfection."

He finds confirmation of this perspective in his reading of *Yirimiyahu* 9:22–23. While humans often make the mistake of relishing lesser perfections, the prophet warns us to glory only in knowledge of God, the height of intellectual perfection.

Had he stopped here, Rambam would have conformed fully to the expectations of those who stress his philosophical side, his belief that intellectual accomplishment, how we mold our minds, is the sole standard by which to evaluate success in life. Instead, Rambam continues, ostensibly for the sake of completeness, since he has mentioned the verse and its wondrous truths, he will "complete the exposition of what it includes."

What's Beyond Intellectual Perfection?

He needs to be complete because the verse[6] does not stop at the words "achieve insight and know Me"; it goes on to name specific

---

6. The verses read:

כה אמר ה': אל יתהלל חכם בחכמתו, אל יתהלל גבור בגבורתו, אל יתהלל

עשיר בעשרו: כי אם בזאת יתהלל המתהלל, השכל וידע אותי כי אני ה' עושה

חסד משפט וצדקה בארץ כי באלה חפצתי נאם ה'.

Thus says the Lord: Let not the wise man glory in his wisdom, let not the mighty man glory in his might, let not the wealthy man glory in his wealth; but let him that glory glory in this that he achieves insight and knows me [note: I have reinterpreted the verb *haskel* as I believe it means more, at least to Rambam, than just to understand], for I am the Lord Who exercises lovingkindness, justice, and righteousness in the Earth, for in these I delight, says the Lord.

aspects of God, those of His "actions" in the world. For Rambam, the verse means that knowing God will lead human beings to similar ways, performing acts of lovingkindness, righteousness, and judgment (not coincidentally, the terms he defined in Chapter 53). The person who reaches the highest perfection, in other words, will have understood as much about God and His actions in the world as possible and will then act in like manner.

Rambam's concern with action has puzzled many of his students, medieval and modern, since he elsewhere focuses so strongly on the intellect. Having argued that politics and morality are lower forms of perfection than the intellectual, why would he then require such actions of the person who has achieved all the perfections?

The question has been discussed numerous times, and any survey of the answers is beyond my scope or interest. In my reading, though (and others agree), Rambam is espousing exactly the kind of process I have been identifying as the essential goal of the religion. The perfect person will come to understand God's attributes of Action, either by studying the universe, the *mitzvot* (which perfect the body, the soul, and the polity), or, likely, both. Once understood, the person will act on them, a way of live-testing our understanding of God. *Mitzvot* are not an end, they are a means — and, I believe, a more easily effective means — to developing our understanding of God, opening the way to imitate God productively.[7]

Here too, then, Rambam views Torah and *mitzvot*, God's exactly defined and heteronomously imposed rules, as building blocks of a greater freedom, an individualistic and idiosyncratic adventure in imitating the God we understand.

---

7. Rambam may have meant that such actions then teach us even more about God — as we try to run the world as God would, our failures and successes help us improve our model, thus feeding back to improve our intellectual perfection.

Derashot haRan

Perhaps rationalists are prone to such a perspective, so that Rambam's ideas do not prove much. That we find similar ideas emanating from the less philosophical pen of R. Nissim Gerondi, Ran, gives more reason to recognize that this is simply the way Judaism views itself.

In two of his *derashot*, or sermons,[8] Ran speaks of human input into the world in exactly the kind of creative way we have been discussing. He portrays both the king and the Sages as empowered and required to use their own ingenuity and reasoning to legislate in ways that insure that the Torah's overall goals are successfully achieved. That process inherently involves understanding the system and its goals fully and thoroughly, but then going beyond the clearly declared rules of the system to articulate further ways of achieving those goals.

Making Ran's position even more surprising, he held that the observances of the Torah function metaphysically to increase and enhance God's presence in the world. If so, his acceptance of the importance of human intellect in that process evinces a sense of autonomy even more significant than the one I have been trying to articulate; in Ran's view, human beings are supposed to partner with God in molding the world in His image.

Filling in the Blanks: Ran's View of Jewish Monarchy

Ran thinks the highest form of that partnership resides with *Hazal*, the Sages of tradition, but before we get there, we can see that his view of the king already points to the value and necessity of human input. In the eleventh *Derasha*, Ran takes for granted

---

8. In the eleventh and the thirteenth sermons, as published in L. Feldman's 2003 Mossad haRav Kook edition of the *Derashot*. In his earlier edition (Jerusalem, 1977), Professor Feldman placed the "thirteenth" sermon after the fifth, titling it the "other" sermon, as had been the practice in earlier editions. We will give page numbers for both editions in our footnotes.

that the system of justice set up by the Torah cannot produce a working society. In his example, the Torah's burdensome evidentiary rules ensure that justice never miscarries, but would lead to anarchy, since no one could be convicted of a crime.

The king steps into that void. His job, like that of the kings of other nations, is to insure that society runs well and smoothly; in doing so, he does not need to adhere completely to the Torah's regulations. The king can decide to convict criminals, for example, based on one witness or circumstantial evidence, despite that not constituting proof in Torah law.

That might be brushed aside as addressing a practical flaw, not an ideological commitment to creative adaptation. Since governments cannot run only by Torah law, we might think Ran is saying the Torah threw in a fix-it, a meta-systemic figure who could insure its continued healthy functioning.

Two of Ran's comments show that that is too minimal an expression of his view. First, Ran tells us that *all* the Torah's laws aim at increasing God's presence in society. While Torah law may sometimes or often apply in practice, its *purpose* is to create a system in which God is openly present.

Torah law's inability to run a working society is no failure, since that was never its goal. For Ran, acquitting a man when rabbinic courts find insufficient evidence achieves the same Torah value as finding him guilty, since both will have brought a greater infusion of God's presence into society. True, the king will then need to deal with the criminal, but the positive accomplishment of the court's actions is independent of its social effectiveness.

That already suggests that the king is more than a stopgap; he is a separate and necessary part of a system where responsibilities are divided. Hazal and Torah law bring God into the world, the king keeps that world in working order. His lack of obvious fetters already invests his human capacities with significance, shows us at least one person whose autonomous input into the world was vital and necessary to God's picture of how that world should work.

The Scroll on the King: Not Complete Autonomy

The king's obligation to carry a Torah scroll and to read from it all the days of his life, for Ran, reminds the king of the limits to his autonomy, tells him he is not some kind of rogue operative on the outskirts of Torah society. Ran cannot read the obligation in its most obvious way — that the Torah wanted to insure the king would not get so caught up in his power as to ignore or disobey Torah law — since he specifically granted the king the right and responsibility to violate the Torah when necessary for society to work.

Ran explains this by noting there are two ways to violate a system's rules, as rebellion against the system or as a "breaking in order to repair," a way to help the system continue to function when circumstances get in the way. The obligation to carry and read from the Torah reminds the king that he needs always to operate the second way, doing his best to see to it that the rules he promulgates foster increased fear of God in himself and in the populace, supporting the Torah system rather than getting away from it.

Following Ran's logic and applying it to a modern society shows that he would need more people than just the king to think in this way. While Ran may have thought that the kings of old could handle all the affairs of state on their own, our experience of government makes it clear that when the Jewish monarchy is restored, the king will need legions of advisers to help consider the range of issues involved in making a working society. Given Ran's view of the king's job, each of those advisers (and all of their analysts) will need to be similarly immersed in Torah, to know how to maintain its values even as the king has to abrogate *halachah* itself.[9]

---

9. Ran also assumes that in the absence of a king, the Sages might be allowed to operate in this way, expanding the group of people who would need to learn to think and operate this way.

One Giant Step for Mankind

Ran's prescriptions for *Hazal* show an even greater role for human ingenuity. Most famously, Ran understands the Talmud to say that we are required to follow the majority opinion even where it contradicts God's. *Hazal* do their best to understand what God wants, and we follow their view, even if they end up erring.

That would be remarkable, but perhaps the only feasible way to operate; it is more remarkable for Ran to say it because of his belief that each commandment plays a specific metaphysical role in shaping our lives; error thus changes not only from what God wants, but damages the metaphysics of the world. To reconcile how the system could tolerate such errors, Ran claims God valued human determination of the law so highly, it *overrode* the metaphysical loss.

Insistent pragmatists might still read these statements as technical and practical, necessary operating mechanisms for a system that does not rely on prophecy for all truth. In another place, though, Ran asserts that the role of the rabbis in shaping the system is weightier than that of the original Torah itself. Discussing the importance of following rabbinic rules, Ran notes Talmudic assertions that the words of the rabbis are more valuable than those of the prophets, and also accepts the view of R. Yohanan, *Gittin* 6ob, that the majority of the Torah is Oral and the minority Written.

Lest we think that the term Oral here refers only to that which was specifically handed down at Sinai (הלכה למשה מסיני), Ran lists for us what he includes in that term: that which came down orally at Sinai, the decrees the Sages promulgate to protect Torah law (arguably technical rather than creative), and "מה שיבררו בכוונת התורה שלא ימצאו לו סמך מן התורה, that which they clarify in the intent of the Torah, for which they find no [direct scriptural] support in the Torah."[10]

That last category again brings us where we have been going

---

10. 90 (526).

throughout these posts, to the expectation that the system of *halachah* would not remain static, or even only be added to in the technical form of protective measures. A part of *Hazal's* expected function was that they would develop a mastery of the system so extensive they would spot situations that called for legislation, despite the Torah itself not having covered it. This applied to both the positive and negative; Ran might easily see the holidays of Purim and Hanukkah as examples of this phenomenon.

Our brief discussion of Ran shows that Rambam's perspective was not solely for the philosophically minded. Both in the realm of Torah (for *Hazal* and their students) and outside of it (for the king and his advisers), Ran, too, thinks human beings were to understand God's system, expressed both by the Torah and the world, find places where the system was not yet functioning as fully as possible, and then conceive, legislate, and actualize rules that increase the system's ability to foster its goals.

Ran's view of *mitzvot* as teaching the king and *Hazal* where and how to make their contributions captures the balance between overreliance and underreliance on *mitzvot* that has too often eluded others who discuss the issue. *Mitzvot* are neither the endpoint of one's service nor dispensable starter-practices. Rather, *mitzvot* build the framework within which humans must fit their own creativity.

And so on, and so on, וכהנה וכהנה; I could add more and more examples, but belaboring the point will add little to what I have already demonstrated so many times, that God wants more than technical observance, that רחמנא לבא בעי, that we are supposed to be putting our heart — by which I mean our creative and autonomous input — into our relationship with God.

As I said at the outset, all of this might be interesting as a set of theoretical propositions, but my own concern is practical ramifications. In the concluding chapters, I am finally ready to take up how a full acceptance of the ideas I have shared here would reshape central aspects of our personal and communal Jewish lives.

Chapter 22

Where Does *We're Missing the Point* and the *Necessity of Autonomy* Take Us?

I have claimed so far that Judaism is constructed differently than ordinary experience suggests. Rather than a set of rituals Jews must observe, I have argued that the religion unequivocally emphasizes that those rituals are meant to build and sustain an awareness of God; of God's role in the past, present, and future; and of our need to mold ourselves to be as similar to that God as humanly possible.

While many of the ways to do that are specifically legislated, others are left to our own imaginations and intuitions. In the last few chapters, I want to share some of the ways in which the conclusions we have reached here seem to me to necessitate significant change in how Jews lead their lives.

The Mission and Character Development

One easy place to see the effects of these ideas is in our sense of the proper character development of a Jew. At all moments of life, Jews are required to be striving to be more God-like. Many, many people strive to improve themselves, but a Jew seeks to do it in two importantly different ways. First, we do not primarily do it because we owe it to ourselves or our families; we do it because God told us to. That difference feeds the second, that the parameters for what constitutes self-improvement were set long ago by God and Jewish tradition; we each adopt a personal form of that self-improvement, but do not define it anew.

I would add that this character development always has another element, the notion that we are partnering with God in furthering the perfection of the world God created. Whereas an ordinary human visits a friend who is ill as an expression of friendship, Jews see friendship, with full appreciation of the value and human dignity of the sick friend, as one among many ways to establish a world that operates as God wants.

When God visited Abraham to model the act, informed him of the impending destruction of Sodom to teach him about charity and justice (and, as we have seen, the human ability to offer prayers to alter the proposed future), and later revealed a longer list of Attributes to Moses at Sinai, God was giving Jews the great gift of a blueprint of how we can mold ourselves to be more God-like.

That means that a first part of Jewishness is that each individual see him- or herself as obligated to strive to develop *along certain lines*. Questions of health, financial security, emotional and relational development, and career success all have their place, but should be subordinated to and brought in line with the constant goal of forming ourselves and our characters to be better servants of God. An Orthodox Jew isn't so much one who keeps Shabbat, kosher, and/or other rules and laws; an Orthodox Jew is one who strives, through *halachah* and beyond, to develop a character that is more God-aware, more God-driven, and more God-like. It is a lifelong project, enhanced by all Jewish observances, but cannot be allowed to be lost in the welter of them.

The Jew's View of History

Another example of how Judaism seeks to shape us is in its view of history as saturated with purpose. From the moment of Creation, through the Exodus and the Giving of the Law at Sinai, the Jew must see history as moving — slowly, with many detours and some steps in the wrong direction, but inexorably — to a time when the entire world will recognize the Kingdom of God and act in ways that reflect that awareness. Jewish belief in the coming of the Messiah cannot be only a backup plan reassuring us when life gets too terrible. It is and must be an ever-present awareness of the direction of human history, that we know and long for the end of this movie, although we have not yet figured out how to get there.

That does not free us of the need to worry about the political future and its consequences. But knowing to reject certain scenarios of history as impossible because God has promised they will never occur puts Jews across a conceptual abyss from those who do not accept that perspective. For one example, it would seem to be impossible that global warming would ever get so bad as to wipe out humanity (at least before the arrival of the Messiah); we can worry about whether we are properly working and preserving God's world, and can see global warming as evidence of failure in that regard, but the broader claims made about how it will affect history going forward — when at odds with what we know about the course of human history — are irrelevant to the faithful Jew.

This sense of history should impact day-to-day life in too many possible ways for me to make any specific prescriptions. What I can say is that the God-centered focus of the religion tells us to look at history with questions in mind, such as whether God is intervening in x or y historical event, and, if so, to try to understand the message of that intervention. When we see no such specific interventions, our constant awareness of God's role in history should still remind us to always wonder how our actions, and those of the various communities in which we affiliate, are bringing us closer to or further from the time when God's Kingdom is recognized throughout the world.

A Jew's Perspective of Major Life Choices

Moving from character and history to what might seem more mundane, what we have learned together should show a different take on how Jews approach many of the basic life questions. Where to live, whom to marry, how many children to have, which kinds of material pleasures to enjoy, are all issues where we need to adopt a God-centered perspective. In addition to the usual factors of climate, type of community, whom we fall in love with, how easy or difficult we find child-rearing, how much we enjoy certain activities, Jews need to also always be thinking about how each of these choices contribute to or take away from their relationship with God, their building themselves in a more God-like manner.

This also gives a new rubric within which to consider the choice of a profession. Many if not most Orthodox Jews, I assume, worry about specific *halachic* problems in any career they would enter and try to solve them. But the commandments about relating to God, loving and fearing God, and especially the notion of autonomy, all suggest that we should choose what we spend the bulk of our lives doing by how well it contributes to those goals.

Given the choice, should a Jew be a doctor or a shoemaker? That depends. Both professions, done right, can serve the greater needs of humanity, provide sustenance to support one's other *mitzvah* involvements, and can teach great lessons about how to serve God humbly in this world. Done wrong, each of these (and any other) can be misused and become soul-deadening. The answer, then, is not one or the other — it is the one that, *for that person*, will produce the best overall result.

It is the definition of the words "best overall result" I hope to have changed. While some may assume those words mean the choice that makes the person happiest, gives a good enough salary to allow a certain kind of lifestyle, or, from a more explicitly religious perspective, the maximum time to study Torah, I am suggesting here that the basic point of the religion is to define "best result" as that which leads to a life that allows for the fullest picture of service of God. That will likely include some vacation time, some kind of a home and other material needs, and should certainly include the study of Torah, but much more besides.

Jewish Morality and Religiosity — Not Just Pots and *Mikveh*

In life in general and in whichever career the Jew chooses — or even if events thrust a choice upon him or her — there will be opportunities for expressing, to oneself or to others, how differently we see the world. Moral dilemmas, for example, are opportunities to notice that while ordinary people try to come to an understanding of the right and wrong of the situation, the Jew tries to understand what God most wants.

That is sometimes black and white — don't eat the pork — but many times it is a question of better and worse, and the framing of the question each time such issues arise is itself an important step in the service of God, part of always having love and awe of God in mind.

In this scheme, incidentally, a great imbalance of Jewish attitudes would be rectified. As I said earlier, many Orthodox Jews view their *religious* lives as the time when they are eating kosher food, studying Torah, attending synagogue, and other conspicuously ritual activities. In fact, though, remembering the goal of becoming more like God and its related *mitzvot* tells us that *all* of how we live reflects our current state of religiosity and is meant to be experienced as such.

If I choose to live in a certain neighborhood because it will foster my connection to God rather than stunt it, I have made, to a certain extent, all of my living circumstances an act of worship of God. If I choose one field over another because it offers better opportunities to connect with the Creator, I have turned all those moments — or many of them — into expressions of my relationship with God. And so on.

I write those words fearing they sound fluffy or inexact. To avoid that, I turn now to the center of Jewish life, *halachah* and the observance of *mitzvot*, where many of these issues should be fully alive and yet are not. For one striking example, the author of *Mishnah Berurah*, a commentary on *Shulchan Aruch*, pauses in his commentary, 156:4 to note, at length, a dozen *mitzvot* important to Jewish experience *not addressed* by *Shulchan Aruch*. *Mishnah Berurah* is a popular work of *halachah* often referred to, yet I do not recall ever hearing that note discussed, let alone repeatedly referred to as central to a proper Jewish experience.

This might be understandable within *yeshivot*, where the curriculum strives to cover the entire range of Torah, so that there might be an expectation that students will be exposed to all the ideas of the religion, including those raised here. In the community at large, this is less true. There, the discussion is mostly or solely of those *mitzvot* and *halachot* that can be defined exactly and specifically, leaving the more loosely defined obligations unreviewed.

I once heard the late Nechama Leibowitz bemoan this educational reality — in her example, the presentation of *Parashat Mishpatim* in school involves large amounts of time spent discussing the laws of an עבד עברי, a Jew who becomes an indentured servant, and almost no time discussing the laws of truth-telling, despite the explicit verse, מדבר שקר תרחק, you shall stay far from falsehood. She explained it as a function of the former topic being complicated, whereas the latter seems simple.

But, as I noted earlier, behavior is belief. When we fill our speech about *halachah* with only the areas where tradition has ruled definitively, we teach ourselves and those around us that *that* is when we are being Jewish, when we wear the prayer shawl, study the Torah, make the *Kiddush*, sit in the *sukkah*.

That is true, but so are we being Jewish when we tell the truth because God's seal is truth; when we conquer our anger because we believe God wants us to learn to be more patient; when we invest in a company because, aside from whether it will make money, we think it will improve the world.

I could take each of the propositions in the earlier chapters and expand upon them to show how this works in practice, but I fear being repetitive. The clear point is that current *halachic* practice often focuses on real yet lesser issues, allowing us not only to lose the forest, but to pay attention to the smaller trees while neglecting the biggest ones. It is not that we are too *halachic* and not theological or *hashkafic* enough (although we may be), it is that even our awareness of *halachah* neglects issues of central importance.

If we find ourselves spending the bulk of our religious efforts ensuring that we have kosher animals, birds, and fish to eat; that we avoid violating the prohibitions of the Sabbath, Yom Kippur, and holidays without caring about the positive content of those days; that we have what to eat on Passover without considering what freedom it means to inculcate in us; we need to rethink the extent to which our lives are succeeding at the *basic* point of the religion, let alone its ideal expression.

Even if we spend our time studying Torah, praying, and visiting the sick, we might still need to check that we are doing so out of a sense of obligation to and connection with God. People can become accustomed to any sequence of actions and make them an end of their own, forgetting the larger framework into which they were supposed to be integrated.

Much as R. Yisrael Salanter slaved to rejuvenate awareness of character issues in Judaism, and the Chafetz Chayim focused on matters of slanderous speech, I am suggesting we expand their model to insure that all the central parts of Judaism are at the top of our agenda.

Such a shift would yield another dividend that leads us to the next topic. Since many of the areas of *halachah* I discuss here have yet to be as exactly codified as others, and perhaps are immune to such exact codification, the experience of the inexactness of the answers to questions in these areas would remind Jews of another important aspect of Orthodoxy, its balance of pluralism, tolerance, and absolutism.

Chapter 23

Pluralism and Charity

In multicultural Western society, pluralism is understood to mean we should accept just about all ways of life as legitimate options. Orthodoxy's insistence that there are objective standards of right and wrong sits poorly with this ideology, since it means that we are less open to different ways of life or approaches to the world.

In confronting the challenge this constitutes, some Orthodox Jews celebrate and exaggerate our closed-off stance, proud of the moral certainty they see it producing, especially as compared to the rudderlessness of Western culture. Others, convinced of the fundamental truth and value of openness, chafe at what they see as the religion's intolerance; to free themselves, they seek to expand the bounds of Orthodox pluralism.

I believe our discussion has shown support for each side. In some places, Judaism speaks unequivocally, with no room to accept diverging views. Perhaps even more often, there are areas of legitimate and lasting debate about which view is correct, and, lastly, areas where Judaism is in fact pluralistic, recognizing many equally valid views. As I lay out those categories, I hope we will see how Judaism is sometimes absolutist,[1] sometimes tolerant,

---

1. Some claim that even our absolutism is not so absolute, since we may not be obligated to bring others to our perspective. On this issue, see M. Broyde, "The Obligation of Jews to Seek Observance of Noahide Laws by Gentiles: A Theoretical Review" in D. Shatz, C. Waxman, and N. Diament, eds., *Tikkun Olam: Social Responsibility in Jewish Thought and Law* (Rowman & Littlefield, 1997). While R. Broyde may be right technically, it seems clear to me that if we are in possession of a truth that affects the lives of others, how could we not try to make them

and sometimes fully pluralistic. This, in turn, will remind us of our need to approach each of those kinds of issues from the proper perspective.

Absolute Right and Wrong: An Internal Value

Orthodox Jews cannot be pluralistic about central issues we have discussed here, such as the existence of God, the historicity of the Exodus and the Giving of the Torah, or the significance of idolatry or sexual immorality. We can tolerate other views on these issues as a practical matter, but we must remind ourselves that we wait for a time when we can be more open about those beliefs, and bring the world to recognize the truths we know. In such instances, as well, we must especially reiterate, at least inside our heads, our implacable opposition to any view that runs counter to these fundamental aspects of Jewish consciousness.

This need to keep in touch with our personal values as we operate in a society that makes very different assumptions reminds me of the story Elie Wiesel includes as the frontispiece to one of his books, of a preacher who goes to Sodom in the hopes of helping them repent their evil ways. The first day he draws a huge crowd, but as time goes on and his message stays the same, the audience dwindles, until he is standing on his soapbox, speaking to no one.

A boy, still too young to be indifferent to his plight, asks him why he continues to preach when no one is listening. Replies the preacher, "I used to preach to convince them of what I believe; now I preach to remind myself of what I believe." (The preacher's reasons for staying in Sodom do not appear in the story; perhaps he had developed commitments and attachments to family, profession, or financial assets he could not see himself relinquishing.)

There are many politically sensitive issues for which the answer would seem to be the same — Jews today might find themselves

---

aware of it? Regardless of obligation, if you had a way to make others aware of the risks of smoking, high blood pressure, or similar physical phenomena, would you not?

unable to speak up about the oppression of the poor, the corruption of power, wrongful sexuality, assisted suicide, evolution and the role of God in that process, and so on and so on. On all these occasions, though, we must remember to register our vigorous disagreement at least internally, lest we lose sight of the way of life God has given us.

The Dangers of Absolutism

At the other extreme, we can imagine Jews who overstate what the religion requires, who ignore or fail to realize the many times we are left with multiple valid options, such as in choosing a profession or which acts of kindness to perform. Where some might assume God wants all Jews either to study Torah full-time, to become a doctor, lawyer, or accountant, and to visit the sick, clothe the naked, or feed the hungry, we should again correct the misimpression, reminding ourselves that God created a rich world with many right ways to contribute to its smooth functioning, both professionally and in our *mitzvah* acts.

In between, there are the areas where we can be tolerant. On such issues, we might disagree with others, we might see them as wrong, and yet still recognize and respect that they arrived at their views through a legitimate process, however erroneous we assume it to be. The simple example is when reputable *halachic* authorities come out on different sides of an issue. Here, as I follow my own *halachic* authority, I likely see those following the other view as wrong or in error, but fully tolerable error.[2]

---

2. To some extent, our pluralism depends on our understanding of *Eruvin* 13b, אלו ואלו דברי אלוקים חיים, these and these are words of the Living God. As Avi Sagi documents in his *Elu va Elu: A Study in the Nature of Halachic Discourse* (Tel Aviv, 1996), most *rishonim* understood the statement to mean that while one side was right and one wrong, both were praiseworthy for having attempted to understand God's Will, and that God allowed us to follow the majority, wrong as it might be. For these authorities, *halachic* disagreements were a clear example of tolerance, not pluralism. Later, more kabbalistically influenced writers

The issue of pluralism and tolerance from an Orthodox perspective can thus guide much of our internal conversation as we interact with others. How much of that mental chatter we share with those around us depends on the person and the situation, but the sifting of ideas by whether we reject, disagree with, or accept them should be one characteristic aspect of the essential Orthodox life. In my experience, it often is not.

It's Not Your Money:[3] Making Charitable Contributions with the Required Care

The same loss of perspective is an issue for our charitable endeavors. The overall shape and thrust of charitable giving is a complicated topic since it touches on money, one of the last taboos of American society, but a few thoughts seem relevant in the context of applying the ideas we have studied.[4]

While I noted earlier that charity necessitates deep personal choice, there are also better, worse, and wrong choices about charity, especially in a world where both religious energy and money are limited.[5] Let me review a few.

---

suggested the phrase meant that both perspectives in fact drank of some larger truth. If so, the two sides to a *halachic* debate could view each other pluralistically rather than tolerantly.

3. See *Avot* 3:7.

4. For a recent *halachic* work on the topic, see יסודי צדקה, *Foundations of Charity*, a 600-page discussion by R. Menachem Kasdan. I have not yet had time to consult it; more to the point, I doubt many people will put in the time and effort to understand the topic in the depth and sophistication with which he presents it.

5. *Shulchan Aruch, Yoreh Deah* 249:1 imagines a person wealthy enough to provide all the needs of the relevant poor. In a different vein, Reynold Levy, *Yours for the Asking*, assumes that wealthy people have plenty to give, and the challenge for fundraisers is to convince them to open their wallets further. This may be true, but should not be confused with the right to dispense those monies with careful thought as to where and how we give — in a globalized world, even the wealthiest's charity does not suffice. The Bill and Melinda Gates Foundation, which disburses

In a religion where God sits at the center, our giving should centrally focus on supporting those people and advancing those causes and institutions that help us and others build a better relationship with God, that help us and others become more God-like (including, especially, by performing the kinds of kindnesses Scripture portrays God as performing, but also by avoiding wrong beliefs about the natural and metaphysical workings of the world and wrongful sexuality), and further the spread of awareness of God in the world.

That leaves flexibility for personal decisions while ruling out some decisions as illegitimate. What it seems to require is that charity should be given not just to worthy causes, but primarily to those that match our sense of personal mission.[6] Some otherwise laudable institutions may promote a different worldview than ours; while *Gittin* 61a already enjoins us to give even to idolatrous causes in the name of fostering good social relations, we should also keep in mind the tone of our giving as a whole.

For example, if a Jew believes in God yet gives the bulk of his or her charitable dollars to poor people who insist on a pagan worldview, or to institutions that promote at best an agnostic and often a stridently atheistic view of the world (such as many modern universities); or, in reverse, if a Jew who believes in the State of Israel as a positive historical development gives significantly to institutions that view that State as at best tolerable; those choices need re-examining for whether they lose sight of what our religious actions are supposed to be about.[7] Since charity is an

---

billions of dollars a year in charity, nonetheless budgets its giving carefully and with an eye towards maximal impact. The Orthodox world should be doing no less.

6. My teacher, R. Lichtenstein, has published a more lengthy discussion of this issue in *Tradition* 42;4, Winter 2009. His conclusions are, I think, largely similar to mine here.

7. A friend once told of receiving a fundraising call from an elementary school from a different community, with a different outlook than his own. He showed the presence of mind to say, "I'm glad you called, because I was just about to call you to support my local school." It may

extension of overall religiosity, it should express the same values and goals as in the rest of our lives.[8]

Here too, we would need to avoid the dangers of absolutism. Aligning charitable giving with our values and beliefs is not the same as rigidly donating only to those organizations that meet all our criteria; just as we recognize the importance of minor *mitzvot*, which do not in and of themselves express all the broader ideals of the religion, many charitable causes can be valuable even if not indispensable. All I mean here is that we must ensure that the broad outlines of our giving further our central concerns, not lose sight of them in a mass of other causes and goals we have taken on.

The Proper Frugality of Charitable Institutions

The difficult calculations such a thought process requires of us would seem to also change our attitude about how we expect charitable funds to be spent. In a world of abundance, where there is enough money for anything we want, another new and expensive building presents no problem. And, to be fair, such a building is often necessary to an endeavor's success. To support a worthy institution of learning, or a research institute, or a mental-health clinic, only to see it fail because of its ugly or outdated facilities is

---

be a stereotype, but it seems true that many left-wing Jews of various levels of affiliation support institutions outside their perspective of Judaism — educational, cultural, and otherwise — to a greater extent than others. It seems to me that if an institution promotes a differing view of how the world should look, people should generally look elsewhere for institutions with whom they share core concerns.

8. I think that is the meaning of the story of R. Yehudah haNasi resisting supporting עמי הארץ, *amei ha-aretz*, in famine years, *Bava Batra* 8a; when we translate *amei ha-aretz* as ignoramuses, his position sounds indefensible, but we need to remember that in that era, it referred to those *opposed* to the rabbis' attempts to spread an authentic religiosity, not just those uneducated in the Rabbis' worldview and ideas. R. Yehudah haNasi saw no reason to support such people; had they changed their minds, I assume he would have gladly helped them as well.

at least as foolish as wasting money on extravagances. The Temple was famously beautiful and avoided the appearance of concerns about money.[9]

But each extravagance needs to be weighed. The money spent on one cause cannot be spent on another; even as this must not translate into a miserly doling out of each charitable dollar with begrudging care (the perfect is the enemy of the good), it does obligate individuals and communities to consider where they are sending their charity and how the institutions are spending them. Such budgeting may not, in the end, alter actual giving, but the repeated self-evaluation will ensure that money is a living out of the ideals each donor carries internally.

Two more areas that call for some restoration of values, then, are our sense of pluralism and our charitable giving. For the first, I argued that we should evaluate ideas along three lines — whether they contradict our irreducible minimum of right and wrong; are legitimate perspectives even if we personally disagree with them; or are views that may not be my cup of tea, but as right as anything I am choosing.

For charity, I argued for a heightened sense that giving is supposed to be an extension of our ideals, that our profile of causes should match the ways in which we hope to improve the world. Making these difficult choices would also, I suggested, lead to a more careful budgeting of charitable dollars.

---

9. See, e.g., *Ketubbot* 106b, אין עניות במקום עשירות, and other citations of this phrase.

Chapter 24

Rethinking Jewish Education

The ideals of Judaism are transmitted in various places, but none so important as home, school, and synagogue. I hope all that I have written until now has contributed to the thought process of those who are in the home fronts of the religion, but I want to say something more specific about those other two institutions.

As the primary location of childhood education — where children spend more of their waking time from ages five and up than any other place, including home — schools' success at transmitting even the minimal picture of Judaism I have laid out here should be a matter of concern. To bring that concern to a feverish enough pitch to ready us for change, let me first note how problematic school has become in non-Jewish contexts.

One deep problem lies in schools' setting goals whose value is unclear to many, especially students. For example, Michael Bradley, a child psychologist, was trying to explain school to teen readers of his *Yes, Your Parents Are Crazy*. Describing what school is not, Bradley writes:

> School is definitely not relevant (useful), at least not in the way that parents seem to think it is. Most of the subjects you learn in high school *you'll never use as a grown up* [emphasis added]... As an adult, you might end up using some of your high-school courses, but, at best, most of what you learn is forgotten fast and forever after the final exam...[1]

---

1. Michael J. Bradley, *Yes, Your Parents Are Crazy* (Harbor Press: Gig Harbor, WA, 2004), p. 266. Bradley, in my view, correctly diagnoses how this happened: From being institutions that served a select population,

Bradley argues the value of school lies in the discipline it gives,[2] a sentiment echoed by some Jewish educators as well.[3] While this is a tragic state of affairs in general education, the starting point for many social ills, it is doubly so in Jewish education, where the drain on communal resources and the vital importance of conveying *two* curricula means we cannot allow this state of affairs to continue.

Jewish schools, I believe, exacerbate the problem by striving to accomplish too much in the time they have, with too little awareness of or agreement about educational priorities. For one simple example, schools' constituencies — students, parents, and educational staff — often never come to agreement about the appropriate balance between the General Studies and the Jewish side of those schools. The odds of accomplishing a meaningful education decrease proportionately to the level of confusion about mission.

What School Ought to Be About

While I have spent this book trying to figure out what Judaism should be about, Howard Gardner — whose work in multiple intelligences has begun to percolate into the Jewish educational community — has spent many years considering the same question for school. After reviewing different societies' educational systems, he notes that all, distinct as they were historically and geographically, had two major goals, "the modeling of adult roles and the transmission of cultural values."[4]

---

they became a place for *all* children, without ever adapting their curriculum to that new reality.

2. I once heard the comedian Jerry Seinfeld say the same about his *college* years.

3. I have heard Jewish educators candidly accept the possibility that high schools can do no more than keep students out of harm for four years, and then send them to Israel to really study Torah.

4. H. Gardner, *The Disciplined Mind: Beyond Facts and Standardized Tests, the K-12 Education That Every Child Deserves* (Penguin Books: New York, 2000), p. 28. Student resistance to learning is understandable

By "adult roles," Gardner means the jobs *that* society needs to function. In other words, the goal of education, Jewish or not, is to ready students for adulthood *in the society they inhabit*. By that standard, graduates of Jewish schools should be ready to take their place as adult Jews *in the society they inhabit*.

This is a challenge on the nonspecifically Jewish side of the curriculum, since educators often insist on forcing students to learn material they will never encounter again in an ordinary adult life in the hope of inspiring them to a broader view of the world. There is much value to this — my road to a PhD began with the fortuitous (or God-sent) encounter with an entrancing teacher, R. Dr. Haym Soloveitchik — but we have to weigh the time, effort, and distraction of coercing students to learn subjects in which they have no interest against the possibility of their finding it suddenly fascinating. If students are required to hear "exposure" lectures, or take one or two such courses in their years in high school, that is different than if almost all their courses are irrelevant unless they go into that field.

More important to me here is that by the standard of readying students to be adult Jews, we are failing demonstrably miserably. One simple proof is how essential the post-high school year or years in Israel have become. Were those years a function of a communal recognition that Torah is so important it needs some extra time of its own, the notion would be both unarguable and would say nothing about the schools those students have studied in until now. In that locution, elementary and high schools might have succeeded as much as possible, and yet we would seek further time for Torah study.

Many schools, though, tacitly or explicitly acknowledge that the year in Israel is indispensable because twelve years of schooling have not produced a *basic* readiness for Jewish adulthood. Considering that more children today are being educated for

when they are being forced to perform in subject areas that neither interest them nor have any bearing on their future lives.

longer than ever in history, this failure rate is dismaying and a shocking use of communal funds.

To adjust Jewish education so that graduates would be ready even to take on the most basic mission of the religion, we must think of the three realms of successful education — affect, skills, and knowledge.

The Affect of a Successful Jewish Education

Affect means the impact of education on the student's persona, his or her interest in living according to the ideas and ideals taught in school. From a Jewish perspective, that means ensuring we not only teach *what* Judaism says, but also imbue students with the commitment to implement what they learn. One benchmark of success would certainly involve the rate at which students act upon the messages transmitted in school.

Unfortunately, it is almost impossible to measure that, because post-graduation choices affect eventual standards of observance. A student with a successful high school experience might lose that in college; while that might signal some failure to convey the importance of supportive environments, we could not assign the school full responsibility for that student's later religious laxity.

At the same time, schools sometimes deserve more credit than the obvious. There are students who leave school with little affect who later encounter situations that bring alive the lessons learned; that later observance should, to some extent, be credited to the school that laid its foundations.

Aside from the difficulty of assessing affect, schools have other tasks they need to include in their agenda, such as conveying the technical skills and knowledge of Jewish adulthood. As we have seen, an adult Jew has many obligations, such as molding his or her character in a Godly fashion, following the *halachic* version of acting honestly in business, laying *tefillin*, buying and shaking a *lulav*, running a kosher kitchen, and others. Graduates of a Jewish school, to fulfill Gardner's ideal of education, need to have the technical knowledge as well as the desire to do so.

Reading Hebrew Texts: A Skill and Its Maintenance

A third side of Jewish education, the one traditionally the focus of Jewish schools but today the bane of educators and students, is the textual, which involves both skills and knowledge. Some of those skills, such as the ability to navigate the yearly *Siddur* or read and understand the *haftarot*, belong as much to the realm of being able to participate in Jewish adulthood as to any ideal of Torah study. Yet anecdotal evidence suggests that few graduates of Jewish high schools can read and understand the *Siddur, haftarot,* or other texts central to a practical experience of Judaism, let alone an intellectual one.

There is also the separate *mitzvah* of *Talmud Torah*. As noted earlier, the Talmud treats the *mitzvah* not only as a commandment, but also as a form of remembering the Giving of the Law at Sinai. Successful Jewish education must prepare students, affectively as well as in skills and knowledge, to fulfill that *mitzvah* as well. A fluent ability to read at least some Hebrew texts thus figures prominently in several scales of Jewish education.

Important and central as these skills might be, Hebrew literacy is vanishing. Educators' ability or will to demand textual proficiency has waned with students' increased resistance. That resistance itself deserves further study, but I suspect it is connected to a loss of the sense of our central commitment to knowing the Torah and its messages and actualizing them in our lives.

These developments are particularly distressing because a generation or two ago, Hebrew proficiency was part of being a Zionist, of feeling connected to Israel; Hebrew language newspapers flourished in early twentieth-century Europe and America. Lest this be seen as only a Zionist issue, I note Rambam's assumption, Commentary on *Avot* 2:1, that the study of Hebrew is itself a *mitzvah*, an example of the "light" *mitzvot* the Mishnah adjures us to treat as seriously as "stringent" ones. Today, though, graduates of "right-wing," non-Zionist schools often have greater textual proficiency than those of more Centrist ones.

The Necessity of Textual Encounter

That may sound exaggerated or overly harsh since people can study Torah in English or by listening to others. Aside from the question of why we feel so sanguine about letting our students forego first-rate Torah study — when we demand first-rate work in other areas, such as university education and professional achievement — let us recall what we have already seen as the basic standard of the *mitzvah*.

The most lenient interpretation required a child to know the Five Books of the Torah, which meant, at a minimum, the ability to read and understand. If so, the most *minimal* standard of Torah education would be for students to be able to open and read, with understanding, any text in the Torah. I feel confident that more than half of graduates of Modern or Centrist Orthodox high schools today cannot meet that standard.

Making it worse, the Talmud assumes that anything written in the Torah itself is known by all Jews, which it indicates with the phrase זיל קרי בי רב, that any schoolchild knows such matters.[5] This would seem to mean we are supposed to have memorized the words of the Torah well enough that they reside actively in our knowledge base, like sports or stock statistics.

Highlighting this insistence on comfort with text, there is a rabbinic obligation to review the entirety of the Five Books each year,[6] a portion a week, twice in the original and once with a

---

5. E.g. *Sanhedrin* 33b and *Shevuot* 14b. I note also the Talmudic practice of asking a child to recite the verse he learned in school that day, פסוק לי פסוקיך, which assumes students learned their verses so well they could recall and recite them at least later that day. That also explains the exception to the principle of מוטב שיהיו שוגגין, not to inform people of mistaken practices they will continue anyway. We assume knowledge of those laws written explicitly in the Torah, however, Rema, *Orach Chayyim* 608:4.

6. *Berachot* 8a-b, codified in *Shulchan Aruch, Orach Chayyim* 285:1.

translation, either Onkelos[7] or Rashi.[8] If so, readying students for Jewish adulthood — the fundamental task of Jewish education, a la Gardner — would seem to necessitate instilling the ability to do that.

Schools also fail to prepare students for other texts they will encounter repeatedly as adults. Most simply, many schools leave students incapable of deciphering *haftarot,* texts that tradition decided should accompany the weekly Torah study in synagogue. Similarly, the *Siddur* in all of its manifestations is opaque to many graduates of Jewish schools — and this, often, despite the school's having *spent* time on study of the *Siddur.* Challenging in language, the yearly liturgy is the text that shapes and accompanies the Jew's conversations with God and binds communities across the world. Knowing how to read these texts is also fundamental to fostering a synagogue life in which prayer involves actual communication between Jews and their Father in heaven.

I harp on these because they are so basic and yet it is not only that schools are not *succeeding* at conveying the literacies and emotional attachments I am recommending, it is that they often do not recognize them as foundational and indispensable.

I once suggested in casual conversation that all students should have read the entirety of Torah (I may have said "with Rashi") by the end of eighth grade. The principal to whom I said this replied, in all seriousness, "It can't be done." While he obviously meant that in the context of the competing priorities schools struggle to balance, I take it as the clearest evidence that we need to recalibrate.

Slower and Steadier: The Key to Success

Once we recognize how fundamental these skill sets and

---

7. *Kiddushin* 49a. See also *Megillah* 3a, which sees Onkelos as the authoritative translation of the Torah, recovering the one used in the time of Ezra.
8. *Orach Chayyim* 285:2.

knowledge bases are, we can question schools' pretense they can accomplish all I have suggested and more, at least if we use their introductions of new literatures as a guide. In schools I know, students are introduced to the *Siddur* in first grade, *Chumash* in second, Rashi in third, *Navi* in fourth, Mishnah in fifth, and Talmud in sixth (or earlier). This pace generally creates a situation where ninety percent of students, at least, are illiterate in six textual milieus by the time they complete six years of Jewish education.

Most of them are, in fact, illiterate in all of those literatures at the end of twelve years as well. Confusing the issue is that in almost every school, the upper echelon of students — the top five to fifteen percent — acquire reasonable to impressive textual skills. This has less to do with educators' success than with these students' innate talents and demonstrate little about how education could or should work.

The struggle with texts points up our loss of awareness of the minimum and indispensable goals of Jewish educations, the ones that must be achieved before moving on to higher aspirations.[9] Just as non-Jewish schools sequence learning in English, math, and sciences, Jewish schools need to return to the appropriate order in mastering texts. I say "return" because *Avot* 5:21, an early statement of Jewish curricular concerns, assumed that mastery of Scripture took five years, of the Oral Law five years, and only then, at age fifteen, would the student take on more sophisticated analysis. This approach was advocated by Maharal, the Vilna Gaon, and niche educators since, such as those who follow the Zylberman method in Israel and abroad.

The common tendency to leapfrog to new texts regardless of whether the old ones have been mastered may be impressive in what it allows students, parents, and schools to say they are

---

9. In this context, I am frustrated to distraction by educators who claim to have found the key to teaching Mishnah or Talmud when those same students cannot yet read more simple and central texts. Whatever that key is, they should be used on basic texts first.

studying, but also counterproductive. Worse, it clouds the sense of mission and commitment the basic texts convey. In the simplest example, spending half or more of a student's weekly Judaic class time to study five or ten pages of Talmud a year — out of a 2200 page corpus — cannot but fail to compete with the need to acquaint the student with crucial other areas of Jewish thought and concern.

Were that time instead used to give a deep and fruitful understanding of the entirety of the Written Torah, as understood by the Oral tradition, it would at least expose students to the range of what God discusses as relevant to a Jewish life. Such localized Talmud study is also unfair to the Talmud itself, in that it necessarily leaves students with a sense of the corpus as narrow, plodding, and overly detailed.

The Political Side of the Problem

Accomplishing what I have called minimal goals would quite possibly fill all the time allotted to Judaic Studies in most schools. Indeed, it is this fact that leads many such schools to reject adjusting their curriculum, since their constituent bodies insist on their course of study including Mishnah, Talmud, *halachah*, Jewish law, Jewish thought, and Jewish history, without regard to the educational realities of those choices. Undeniably important as they are, they also show how the perfect can ruin the good, or in Talmudic terms, תפסת מרובה לא תפסת, loosely translated as "trying for too much gets you nothing."[10]

A more realistic approach seeks to teach only what can be mastered.[11] In one sense, this sounds terrible, since it might

---

10. *Rosh haShanah* 4b. The corollary, my motto here, is תפסת מועט, תפסת, if you take on a manageable amount, you will succeed.
11. Malcolm Gladwell, *Outliers* (Little, Brown: New York, 2008) discusses KIPP (Knowledge Is Power Program) academies, in which students spend significantly more time in school than other public schools. That extra time is not used to teach more, but to ensure that students master each aspect of a subject before moving on to the next one.

mean that by the end of fifth grade students will still be studying *Chumash* and *Siddur*. On the other hand, by using the available time judiciously, these students will *know* the material they have studied. It is a trade-off of a failed ideal for realistic goals that could actually come to fruition.[12]

I will close here because I have come to the end of my unequivocal thoughts. I note, though, that once we remember that Judaism is about developing a relationship with God *through* a set of practices, not about the practices or texts themselves — and that those practices are broader than we often realize — Jewish schools might also see their excessive narrowness in their view of what constitutes a Jewish education. Given that students learn differently and are attracted to different aspects of religiosity, a good Jewish education would grant them the skills, affect, and knowledge to meet minimal standards as well as to develop their own individual foci in their relationship with God.

The details of how to do that are certainly debatable, but the greatest challenge to such creative rethinking of Judaic Studies is sociological, in that many local communities care less about whether students reach valuable goals than that their educations fit a hard-wired picture of what a Jewish school should involve. The first step to changing that is reminding ourselves that we've been missing the point of the necessity of autonomy and then moving to putting those lessons into practice.

---

12. More motivated or talented students can always be offered the opportunity to move faster or move into other literatures — a student already reading the *Siddur* well and with enthusiasm, already skilled at *Chumash* and Rashi (even if he or she has not yet covered it in its entirety) can be introduced to *Navi* earlier, to Mishnah, and, once a meaningful agglomeration of Mishnah has been studied, Talmud and other more advanced texts. My point is not the timing of the sequence, but the discipline of only moving on to a new stage when each old one has been mastered, at least in skills and affect if not yet in knowledge.

Chapter 25

Synagogues as a Place of Worship of God

Schools may prepare children for adulthood, but — as a socio-logical fact rather than an *halachic* one[1] — synagogues are where Jews live out that adulthood. Before even thinking about those institutions, I stress that synagogues are at best an efficient organizing tool for religious life, not the sum total of it. My question here, therefore, is whether synagogues serve their basic function, helping congregants get closer to God.

Complicating the answer, synagogues are also, properly and appropriately, institutions of communal cohesiveness. Building that communal bond and sense of connection involves activities essential to the synagogue's becoming and remaining a venue to which congregants turn for friendship and support. There, too, the limit is that those activities must remain the necessary foundation of a synagogue's communal function, not the sum total of it.

This concern arises in all of a synagogue's official activities. Beginning with the rabbi's various communications with members — speeches, classes, bulletin articles, eulogies, fundraising calls — and expanding throughout its functioning, communities need to check that their synagogue not focus on one area to the

---

1. While *halachic* sources record the importance of synagogue participation (for men, at least), see, e.g., *Shulchan Aruch* 90:9, R. Moses Isserles, in that same paragraph, speaks with equanimity of people who live in places where there is no regular *minyan*. It was not only conceivable, but fully acceptable, to live in a place where public worship would be occasional at best.

detriment of other vital ones. Some rabbis (and their communities) are fascinated by details of ritual *halachah* (even or especially details that do not obviously or immediately connect to broader issues of service of God), some by acts of kindness that mostly create social integration and welfare, and some by political and/ or pastoral activities.[2]

Any and all of these can be positive and important contributions and reflections of a particular community's niche in bringing about a world more focused on God. The danger lies in their becoming ends of their own. Not every sermon can be about ways to better serve God, not every class can discuss big-picture issues, not every communal activity can directly achieve a higher goal; but the sum total of all of those must be directed at the core, central aspects of Judaism, else the community must consider whether it has lost its way.

To phrase it another way, a synagogue in which the majority of congregants see attendance as ways to connect with friends rather than deepen their connection with and understanding of God's law and worldview; in which congregants observe Shabbat or holidays as days to rest and relax from their weekday exertions by sleeping, sunbathing, or hanging out with family; in which congregants see the sum of their mission in life as raising good families and earning a reasonable living is a synagogue that has lost sight of what Judaism is about.

Talking and *Kiddush* Clubs — Freely Admitting I Couldn't Care Less About God

Two phenomena of synagogue life highlight the challenge in

---

2. While hospital visits or *shiva* calls may open the door to a greater relationship, as rabbis often claim, that value is only realized if it actually translates into a changed relationship with God. If all that comes out of it is a better feeling about the rabbi or community, it has to be seen as planted seeds that have not yet sprouted, as a case where the rabbi and synagogue's goals have not yet been fully met.

bringing this truth of the synagogue to life. Consider the issue of talking during services, which has been a problem for hundreds of years, with rabbis bemoaning their inability to rein it in for almost all of that time. In the face of what is so deeply ingrained as to resist generations of protest, many would counsel choosing a wiser battle to fight. Apt though the advice may be, we need to also recognize that talking during services is one of the easiest indications that fear of God does not inhabit a particular place.

When a person or community feels him-, her-, or themselves to be in the presence of God — perhaps the reason so many synagogues place the phrase דע לפני מי אתה עומד, Know before Whom you stand, so prominently —[3] talking to a neighbor should be impossible (as it would be if one had a private audience with the President, let alone the Master of the Universe). The talking is less offensive in and of itself (certainly not of a level of other sins we've discussed) than an example of communicating an underlying apathy to the true goals of synagogue and prayer (which *is* deeply problematic).

The common strategy of asking for quiet as a matter of consideration for others thus misses an opportunity. While that is often effective, phrasing it as a matter of disrespect to God makes a point of reinforcing the synagogue's sense of itself as dedicated to a particular task, not just serving as a convenient gathering point.

This same concern with the synagogue's sense of purpose explains why *Kiddush* clubs should be seen as so dangerous. That members of a synagogue insist on a break in services and time it to the reading of the *haftarah*[4] should irk us for many reasons,

---

3. Taken from *Berachot* 28b, the words are R. Eliezer's response to his students' request that he teach them ארחות חיים, the proper way to live.

4. The need for a break at all is surprising. While Shabbat morning services used to be closer to three hours, they today tend to stay in the two-and-a-half-hour range for main sanctuary services, less for auxiliary ones. I have heard people argue that shorter services would solve both the talking and *Kiddush* clubs problems. My experience suggests otherwise, both in that most people do not want such an abbreviated service and that those who enjoy talking and/or leaving for *Kiddush* will

among the most prominent being that it openly declares a preference for food, drink, and socializing rather than hearing words which, as we have seen, convey central theological messages of the religion. In condoning or turning a blind eye to members' doing so, communities reinforce the sense that they are a social club rather than a group gathered for the service of God.

Taking up the values we have articulated here would give rabbis and communities convenient shorthand for knowing which congregational problems to combat vigorously, how to better triage their activities, and thus how to ensure that their *Mikdash Me'at*, their small sanctuary, merits the maximum possible Divine Presence.

Prayer and the Autonomous Encounter with the Divine

As part of our discussion of synagogues, we should remember what we found regarding prayer. As we saw, Avraham learned and taught us that prayer is an opportunity to go beyond simple acceptance of God's plan to make creative, productive suggestions about how better to shape the future. To be plausible, such ideas have to build on a deep understanding of what God sees as a positive direction for the world, but that standard is flexible enough to leave much room for human input in both conceiving the future and acting to bring it about.

Sadly, as R. Soloveitchik is reported to have said, "The problem with American Jews is that they don't want to *daven* (pray); they want to have *davened*." In many, many synagogues, people show great devotion to attending communal prayer (during the week and on Shabbat) but then fail to actually pray. They open the *Siddur* and recite the words printed there but do not register what they are saying, let alone recognize the invitation to plead their case before God. Prayer, from what Avraham Avinu taught

---

do so anyway (many of them have not been in the synagogue for even an hour before they're leaving for their *Kiddush* club).

us, challenges us to express our individual religious autonomy, to become expert enough at understanding God's goals so as to be able to make creative and original contributions towards achieving them; synagogues today too infrequently convey that perspective.

Halachah as an Extension of the Autonomy of Avraham's Prayer

That same attitude, I maintained, is clear within the realm of שמירת המצוות, the observance of Jewish law, since some of the most important of those laws are defined too generally to give exact guidance in how to fulfill them. By examining a few, and then showing how Rambam and Ran expanded that perspective, I tried to make clear that the proper observance of *halachah* is nothing so lockstep as looking up the law in a book and performing what is written there. That can work for *some mitzvot*, but for many of the most important ones, personal input and creativity is inescapable.

I took pains to stress, and will one more time, that that input is not "freestyle," not whatever a particular individual wants. Rather, within the parameters set by *halachah* and Jewish thought, individuals have choices, all of which are not only reasonable but necessary in shaping the way Jews experience their connection with God.

If so, it is clearly possible to follow *halachah* and yet miss the point. It is tempting to focus on the highly specific areas of *halachah* — blowing *shofar*, shaking a *lulav*, putting on *tefillin* — because those come with the security of knowing we have done something good and important, without getting into the complications of internal experience and recognition of God.

But doing so — and all too many of us do — loses sight of other at least equally important religious obligations. An observant Jew, we all should repeatedly note, loves and fears God, honors his or her parents, gives charity to the extent possible, follows the laws of Shabbat, and in each of those very central areas must necessarily define those *mitzvot* in some kind of personal way, not strictly defined by *halachah*.

Improving the Situation: First Steps for Synagogues and Rabbis

Opportunities to alter this reality abound, especially in a communal setting. Congregants' questions present rabbis with frequent chances to reorient their thinking. Imagine a congregant who appears at public worship only on Shabbatot and holidays, never (to the best of the rabbi's knowledge) studies Torah, is employed in an occupation where complete honesty seems rare, and, perhaps, is engaged in sexually wrongful behavior. This congregant, in mourning for a relative, calls the rabbi to ask about the conduct of that mourning.

As background, remember that the laws of mourning beyond the first day (and possibly only when that first day is both the day of passing and of burial) are rabbinic in origin. Further, many questions regarding mourning, particularly after the first thirty-day period, are guided only by post-Talmudic custom. We need not in any way detract from the importance of adhering to those customs to yet notice that such a person has more pressing religious failings to address.

Not that the rabbi could ever be straightforward in that assessment, but thinking in those terms in that and other situations would help adjust our *halachic* experience. Depending on how far the rabbi could go, he might work to engage the questioner so that he or she walks away understanding that mourning is not about particular practices, but about absorbing a loss in a God-focused and Jewishly faithful way. While refraining from buying new clothing might be an expression of that path, other, perhaps more important, expressions would be turning to God, studying more Torah, becoming more dedicated to *mitzvah* observance, and giving more charity.

One question and answer will not change that person's life, nor a community's, but repeated and conscious consideration of where we place our religious and *halachic* efforts and priorities, the kinds of topics on which we present public lectures, host speakers, and recommend Jewishly-themed books, would be a first step to bringing our *halachic* practice in closer line with what the system itself commands and commends.

Another way to say this is to remember *Yeshayahu* 29:13's protests that the people served God as a מצוות אנשים מלומדה, a rote practice. In his time, that expressed itself in an excessive focus on sacrifices and neglect of the more social *mitzvot*, but the principle applies equally whenever our concern with ritual — especially synagogue-related ritual, since Western culture is so church-focused — causes us to lose sight of other vital ways of serving God. Just as we can and did convert the Temple from a place to encounter God to a ritualistic venue for sacrifice, we can lose sight of what our small Temples are supposed to be — places that give us more direct access to God even in a time of hiddenness. Refocusing, recalibrating, and reconsidering how we structure our communities could, I hope, return those synagogues to their optimal functioning.

A Closing Note:
Citizens of the World

When his Theory of Relativity was not yet fully accepted in the scientific community, Albert Einstein made a perceptive comment: he said that if he were proved wrong, the French would say he was a German, and the Germans would say he was a Jew. Were he proved right, the Germans would claim him as a German, and the French as a citizen of the world. As we think about ourselves in the wake of this extended consideration of the meaning of Judaism, a few last points are worth making.

First, in showing the value of autonomy, I noted that Noahide law is not simply a set of basic moral principles that any rational human being would want to follow. It is, rather, a specific version of morality, one that communicates basic propositions of how God wants all of us to see the world. Those propositions, we should remember, are not only not intuitive, they contradict Western morality at several key points.

That view of the Noahide laws seems to me to capture something more basic about Judaism that has been lost in many circles: it is not a "religion," in the sense that I have my practices, my god, whom I worship in my strange way, and you have yours. It is, rather, a set of claims about the world and its most fundamental underpinnings. To be Jewish is to absorb those claims, to have them suffuse one's persona so fully that they affect all that we do, all that we say, and how we interact with all whom we meet.

To meet someone who consciously and knowingly opposes that which we hold dear — public atheists like Stephen Hawking and Christopher Hitchens come to mind — is not just to see someone with whom we disagree, it is to meet someone who is

251

trying to warp the world, to change it from what it should be. And, in more positive converse, to meet someone who strives to build a world along the same lines as we are is to see a friend of a much deeper level than the bonds of enjoying the same forms of leisure.

As we go about our own religious lives, we should recognize that God has goals for all of us, and that the more minimal set of laws given non-Jews does not free them to do as they wish, although it leaves them much religious autonomy.

Rethinking *Halachah*, Rethinking Jewish Education

All of this brings us, in the end, to the same quandary that has faced prophets, rabbis, thinkers, and educators throughout Jewish history. How do we ensure that people not mistake examples of service of God for the whole of that endeavor? I do not know of anyone who has provided the error-proof answer to that question, but raising it, sensitizing ourselves to it repeatedly, seems a necessary step.

In addition, I have tried to show here that as long as our discussions stay within the realm of defined *halachah*, we miss an essential point, that adhering to the defined was not and is not the essence of what the religion seeks. Even a perfectly balanced observance of all the well-defined *mitzvot* and *halachot* would not yet make us partners in tending God's garden.

That partnership can only occur once we have gone through the rigorous training process of *mitzvot*, continuing to adhere to them carefully and consistently, but also using them as tools to sensitize ourselves to God's goals, כביכול (so to speak), for the world, and to take our place in joining Him to help advance the day when those goals are fully realized, when *Hashem* will be One, and His Name will be One, on earth as in Heaven.